"James Scott Bell is a master of writing c...
teach others, through his books and worksh...
writing ability as gift bestowed upon a chosen few, Bell makes ...
accessible to anyone who is willing to dig deep and put in the time
to learn the craft. I have learned more from James' books than any
writing course, and this book is no exception. As a former teacher
turned novelist, I know how to spot a talented teacher when I see one.
James Scott Bell doesn't just make the cut, he sets the standard."

—KAMI GARCIA, #1 *NEW YORK TIMES, USA TODAY,* AND
INTERNATIONAL BEST-SELLING CO-AUTHOR OF *BEAUTIFUL CREATURES*

"I expect Jim's teaching to inform my writing for years."

—JERRY B. JENKINS, #1 *NEW YORK TIMES* BEST-SELLING AUTHOR

"James Scott Bell is my go-to writing teacher."

—TERRI BLACKSTOCK, *NEW YORK TIMES* BEST-SELLING AUTHOR

"I needed advice before I tried to write a novel. The usual axiom—write
what you know—wasn't helpful. So I turned to James Scott Bell. He
taught me how to structure a great entrance—the equivalent of gliding
down a spiral staircase in a wedding gown—and how to keep the
next 400 pages from becoming as hopelessly tangled as the crumpled
papers and wads of gum in my old desk. My novel sold."

—SARAH PEKKANEN, BEST-SELLING AUTHOR OF *THE OPPOSITE OF ME*

"I am inspired by Bell's enthusiastic approach, and impressed with his
numerous, helpful insights into the craft of storytelling."

—BILL MARSILII, SCREENWRITER, *DEJA VU*

JUST WRITE

CREATING UNFORGETTABLE FICTION
AND A REWARDING WRITING LIFE

JAMES SCOTT BELL

WRITER'S DIGEST
BOOKS

Writer's Digest Books
An imprint of Penguin Random House LLC
penguinrandomhouse.com

Printed in the United States of America

ISBN 978-1-59963-970-3

Edited by Chris Freese
Designed by Alexis Estoye

JUST WRITE

CREATING UNFORGETTABLE FICTION
AND A REWARDING WRITING LIFE

JAMES SCOTT BELL

WRITER'S DIGEST
BOOKS

Writer's Digest Books
An imprint of Penguin Random House LLC
penguinrandomhouse.com

Copyright © 2016 by James Scott Bell

Printed in the United States of America

ISBN 978-1-59963-970-3

Edited by Chris Freese
Designed by Alexis Estoye

ACKNOWLEDGMENTS

I would like to thank Phil Sexton and Rachel Randall of F+W Media for the idea for this book, and Cris Freese and Kimberly Catanzarite for helping me whip it into shape.

Also, a big shout out to my blog mates at Kill Zone (www.killzoneblog.com) and the many thoughtful commenters who make it one of the finest writing craft sites on the Internet.

Most of all, to my wife, Cindy, who demonstrates true love by reading all my work in its early stages, and stays calm.

ABOUT THE AUTHOR

JAMES SCOTT BELL is the author of the number one bestseller for writers, *Plot & Structure*, and numerous thrillers, including, *Romeo's Rules*, *Try Dying*, and *Don't Leave Me*. In addition to his traditional novels, Jim has self-published in a variety of forms. His novella *One More Lie* was the first self-published work to be nominated for an International Thriller Writers Award. He served as the fiction columnist for *Writer's Digest* magazine and has written highly popular craft books, including: *Write Your Novel From the Middle*, *Super Structure*, *The Art of War for Writers*, and *Conflict & Suspense*.

Jim has taught writing at Pepperdine University and at numerous writers conferences in the United States, Canada, Great Britain, Australia, and New Zealand. He attended the University of California, Santa Barbara, where he studied writing with Raymond Carver, and graduated with honors from the University of Southern California Law Center.

Visit his website, www.JamesScottBell.com.

TABLE OF CONTENTS

Introduction

EMBRACE THE FLUX

In one episode of *Downton Abbey*, when it became clear that the old ways of life were on the way out, never to return, Carson the butler mused, "The nature of life is not permanence, but flux."

Right on, Carson. That was true for you, and it's true for us. Especially when it comes to the world of writing.

Because even as I type these words, even as I turn this manuscript in to my wonderful editor at Writer's Digest Books, there is no question that the publishing landscape will be different once this book is available to readers.

Because change is the new normal.

It was never like this in the "old days" (like, before 2007).

The book industry went about things in pretty much the same way for three hundred years. Large companies were in control of the production of paper books. The only way to get a book into wide circulation was to have it published by one of these companies. Writers who hoped to make a living at their craft had only one place to go, and usually that was an outfit in New York.

Along the way, an insatiable reading habit formed among the evermore-educated populace. To serve that habit, magazines printed on cheap pulp paper became a huge business. Cheap but substantial stories and novellas were made possible by such pulps as *Dime Detective, Black Mask, Weird Tales,* and *Fight Stories.*

And still the writer was beholden to those who controlled the printing presses and distribution channels.

Oh, sure, along the way, a few enterprising authors decided they might like to try doing all this themselves. It may have started with a New England poet by the name of Walt Whitman. He paid for the initial printing of his volume of poems, *Leaves of Grass.* To help spur sales, Whitman even wrote some glowing reviews of the book under an assumed name (thus inventing the sock puppet).

Mark Twain was another enterprising self-publisher. He even started his own company and took on other authors' books. The company went bust in 1894.

For the most part, those who paid for the publication of their own books were destined to have a garage full of ... their own books.

Bookstores, you see, dealt primarily with the big publishers. The owners of the bookstores wanted to sell a lot of books. So they ordered most of their stock from those publishers who had signed popular authors.

In the 1980s and 1990s, New York publishers opened the bank vaults in a big way for authors they thought would provide hit books. Some—like John Grisham, James Patterson, David Baldacci, and Danielle Steele—delivered home runs time after time.

But there were even more writers who received those huge advances and saw their books tank, which in turn ruined their careers. No other publisher would sign them because they were marked "damaged goods." A few managed to find homes with smaller publishers. Others faded from the scene altogether.

Harsh.

It was also monstrously difficult for a new author to break into traditional publishing, a land I have sometimes called the "Forbidden City." First, they needed an agent to get them access. Then they were subject to a publisher's committee meeting, where one sour note from the marketing department could scotch a book's publication.

At the turn of our century, the publishing landscape was littered with the scattered manuscripts and bodies of writers who never made it past the gatekeepers.

And it seemed that things would ever be thus.

Until the year 2007.

What happened in 2007?

Helen Mirren took home an Academy Award for her performance in *The Queen.*

The San Antonio Spurs swept the Cleveland Cavaliers to win the NBA championship.

Drew Carey replaced Bob Barker on *The Price Is Right.*

And a company by the name of Amazon introduced a little product they called the Kindle.

CHANGING THE GAME FOREVER

The publishing industry's initial reaction to the Kindle was a yawn. Several years before, the market for electronic books had floundered even though Sony was behind it. *Surely,* thought the New York publishing industry, *no one outside of a handful of techno-nerds was going to go for electronic. Real books were printed! They had covers and dust jackets! Print books would remain the preferred reading experience until the Apocalypse!*

But the following year a few enterprising writers began to notice something. Amazon was allowing writers to publish digital books directly. These books were sold through the Amazon online store. A writer did not have to wait, worry, or pay for printing.

And some of these books took off. Writers no one had ever heard of were selling tens of thousands of books.

Still, there was resistance from both publishers and many authors. Publishers sniffed at these offerings as another form of the self-published book, the kind that had always carried a stigma under the old model.

Old school authors who had "paid their dues" were a little miffed that just anyone could "publish" a book! In their opinion, the only way to be a legitimate writer, a real writer, was to go through New York.

Old ways die hard.

Money started to talk. More and more self-publishing writers enjoyed payments sent directly to their bank accounts. Not twice a year, but each month!

Suddenly writers who had been struggling to find a publishing home, and even writers who were traditionally published but had been dropped for lack of sales, were making solid incomes.

A snowball started rolling down a hill.

And out in the ski lodge virtually every writer saw that snowball and wondered, *Could it really be true? Is it really possible to make money, nay, even a living, via self-publishing?*

The answer, we know now, is a resounding *Yes.*

Never before in the history of book publishing—heck, never before in the history of storytelling (and that's a long time)—has there been so much opportunity for writers to find readers and realize actual moolah from their craft.

OLD SCHOOL REMAINS IN SESSION

During this entire sea change, the traditional publishing industry did not go the way of the Dodo. It was still selling books, and bookstores were still buying.

The so-called Big Six publishing companies became the Big Five, as Random House and Penguin merged.

Then the "Bigs" began to adjust to the changing landscape by trying new ways to sell online and by making alliances with Internet start-ups.

The only thing that was clear was what old Carson observed: flux. Which is both a challenge and a blessing for fiction writers.

The challenge is to keep going, to keep writing and producing, even when you're not sure where all that writing is going to end up.

The flux isn't going away, so you've got to embrace it.

> "The writer who is a real writer is a rebel who never stops."
> —WILLIAM SAROYAN

But with that challenge is a gift: the assurance that there will never be only one road again. There will never be only one way to get your writing out there to the people to whom it matters most—the readers.

And what do those readers want?

They want a story to carry them away. They want to be transported into a dream.

That never changes. That's what you can hang onto as a writer.

In 1926, after five intense years of learning his craft and pounding out stories, a practicing lawyer who wanted to write fiction wrote this in his journal:

> My own approach ... is different from that of the critics. I am a writer. I serve the reading public. The reading public is my master.

His name was Erle Stanley Gardner, the creator of the iconic series character Perry Mason, and he would go on to become one of the best-selling writers of all time.

After his success was established, he wrote a letter to one of his editors, Arthur E. Scott, and said this:

> In my stories I try to figure myself as a prospective buyer of a magazine standing in front of a hotel newsstand. Would my story title make me pick up the magazine to look at it? Would the first hasty glance through the story make me buy the magazine, and would a reading of the yarn make me a regular subscriber?

So one might be tempted here to type the old cliché: The more things change, the more they stay the same. But since I avoid clichés like the plague, I shan't be the one to do it.

Instead I say, embrace the flux, which is here to stay. And write stories that transport readers, who always desire the dream.

And when you have doubts (as all writers do), remember one thing above all, the *summum bonum,* your permanent marching orders in this marvelous craft of telling stories:

Just write.

As long as you do that, you're never out of the game.

USING THIS BOOK

In Part I: Unforgettable Fiction, I give you some guerilla writing tips. There are two kinds of writing advice writers need to absorb:

1. Do the things readers like.
2. Don't do the things readers don't like.

You'll find both in this section. Start absorbing.

In Part II: A Rewarding Writing Life, we'll cover the living of the writer's life. Which means you will write as long as you live. Why wouldn't you? There is no forced retirement for writers, no getting fired. My rules for the writing life are as follows:

1. Produce the words.
2. Keep growing in the craft.
3. Produce more words.
4. Take care of yourself.

Upon those four rules this section is built.

Start construction.

Part I

UNFORGETTABLE FICTION

Chapter 1

WHAT READERS WANT

Your readers are of vital importance to your career as a writer. They're the ones who shell out money to read your writing. If you can't entertain them and keep them interested, you'll have a hard time making a career out of writing. There are certain fundamentals of storytelling that you ignore at your peril. This section is designed to help you know better what works for the broad spectrum of readers.

DON'T WRITE STUFF PEOPLE DON'T WANT TO READ

One of the great bon mots in popular cultural history occurred during the 1974 Academy Awards ceremony. David Niven was at the podium when a streaker (an inexplicable fad at the time) sped across the stage.

The unflappable Niven calmly waited for the laughter to die down, and then remarked in his impeccable English accent, "Isn't it fascinating to think that probably the only laugh that man will ever get in his life is by stripping off and showing his shortcomings?"

Thankfully, the streaking fad is kaput. But there are other places where shortcomings are wont to appear.

Some time ago veteran editor Alan Rinzler posted on Writer Unboxed about "issues" writers today are facing. While the post itself was solid, I was more intrigued by one of his comments. Rinzler was asked a question in the comments by none other than super agent Donald Maass. Don wanted to know what the number one shortcoming Rinzler, as a developmental editor, saw in manuscripts. Rinzler posted the following:

> I see disorganized stories of excessive complexity… intrusive narrative voices that come between the reader and the story by inserting ongoing commentary, explanation, and interpretation … a failure to research and do the homework necessary to come up with something truly original and not reinvent the wheel … two-dimensional stereotype characterization … dialogue that all sounds like the same person.

I like this list. Let's take a look at each item.

Disorganized Stories of Excessive Complexity

I once picked up a bit of screenwriting wisdom that applies here. The best movies (and novels) consist of *simple plots about complex characters*. That is, while the plot may contain mystery and twists (as it should), it is, at its core, a basic story with understandable motives. The real meat and originality comes from putting truly complex characters into those stories. The secret to originality can be found in the limitless interior landscape of human beings.

Intrusive Narrative Voices

Learning how to handle exposition—and especially when to leave it out—is one of the most important and early craft challenges. So get to it. My book *Revision & Self-Editing for Publication* has a whole section on this, but here's one tip: Place exposition seamlessly into confrontational dialogue. Instead of this:

> Frank never wanted to have a baby. Not until he was a success as a writer. But Marilyn thought his quest was foolish. After all, it had been five years since he left his job at AIG. Marilyn dearly wanted him to try to get his job back.

Write the confrontation as dialogue:

> "You never wanted a baby, Frank."

"Shut up about that."

"All because of your stupid writing obsession!"

"I'm not obsessed!"

"Oh really? What do you call five years of typing and no money to show for it?"

"Practice!"

"Well, practice time is over. Tomorrow you're going to beg AIG to take you back."

A Failure to Research ... to Come Up with Something Truly Original

Rinzler is talking about the concept stage here, which is foundational. Hard work on fresh concepts will pay off. And remember, freshness isn't just a matter of something "unfamiliar." All plot situations have been done. It's how you dress them up and freshen them that make the difference. Remember *Die Hard?* After it became a hit, we had *Die Hard* on a ship (*Under Siege*) and on a mountain (*Cliffhanger*) and so on. Take a standard romantic comedy about a writer struggling with writer's block and set it in Elizabethan England and you get *Shakespeare in Love*. Heck, take an old dystopian cult plot like *Deathrace 2000*, put it amongst kids and, bingo, you've got *The Hunger Games*.

Two-Dimensional Characters

We all know that flat characters are a drag on an otherwise nice plot idea. Such a waste! As Lajos Egri put it in his classic, *Creative Writing*: "Living, vibrating human beings are still the secret and magic formula of great and enduring writing."

In chapter three I'll give you some tips on fleshing out your characters. For now, be on the lookout for stereotypical characters in your manuscript. It helps to have a beta reader look for the same thing.

Dialogue that All Sounds Like the Same Person

In my workshops I always say the fastest way to improve a manuscript is via dialogue. It's also the fastest way to get an agent or editor to reject you, or readers to give you a yawn. Good, crisp dialogue that's differentiated via character pops. It gives readers confidence that they're dealing with someone who knows the craft.

The place to start, then, is by making sure every character in your cast is unique. I use a "voice journal" for each, a free-form document of the character simply yakking at me. This helps me develop all of my characters until I truly "hear" each one in a singular fashion.

Target these five vital areas in your novel so you don't have to worry about them becoming a problem. The streaking guy at the Oscars couldn't do anything about his own vital area, but you as a writer can make sure your vital areas are in good form.

A BOOK THAT FAILED AND WHAT WE CAN LEARN FROM IT

A number of years ago a genre author of some repute decided to write a "big, important" novel. The publisher got behind him with a campaign, copious blurbs from name authors, and all the trimmings. The subject matter was "ripped from the headlines." The publisher was sure it would be not only a bestseller but a megahit. The writer was certain to move into that rarified air of the best-selling-*plus*-respected author. Movie rights would surely follow, maybe with Clint Eastwood chosen to direct.

But the book sank like a Mafia stoolie in cement shoes.

Despite all the best efforts of the publisher, writer, and publicity department, readers simply did not buy. Word of mouth failed to issue a positive vibe.

I have two things to say about this.

First, I heartily salute this author for making the attempt to do more with his fiction. Writers need to stretch, grow, and challenge themselves. That always brings the risk of failure. And as The Rock once said about trying comedy acting, "I would rather fail being aggressive than being passive."

Second, with this book, the author seemed to throw out all the fundamentals of plot and structure, as if that was *unnecessary* for an *important* novel. As I read the book (it was tough to get past page ten), I kept thinking *Why is he doing this? Why would he make readers slog through so much tedium? Where was the editor?*

The first two pages are especially dreadful. Purple prose, no close point-of-view character, nothing to bond reader with story— it was an attempt to impress by language alone, and it just wasn't good enough to do that.

Too many characters are introduced too soon—and they're introduced in an omniscient narrative voice. I kept wondering *Who am I supposed to care about?* It wasn't until page twenty-one that he gives us a single, close POV. I was relieved, and thought *This is where the book should have started.*

But then the next chapter introduces a completely different POV. And the chapter after that introduced yet another POV. And, yes, the same for the next chapter. This is extremely hard to pull off. The readers have to care about each character or it seems like a waste of our time.

But the caring does not happen because these chapters consist of long slogs of *narrative summary.* Big chunks of backstory bring the already minimal forward motion to a complete standstill.

And all through these chapters, more prose that seemed designed to *impress* rather than *tell a doggone story.*

This is why the novel failed, even with all the blurbs and publicity and push, which brings us to a few lessons:

Readers Have the Final Say

No matter how much marketing you do, or how much publicity and ad buys you're able to garner, readers alone will decide if the book is going to sell. Word of mouth is the great determinant of sales success. If you are writing to impress critics, you may get one or two nods. But won't get your advance repaid or bank account filled.

Hey, Maybe There Are Rules After All

Some writers are fond of saying, "There are no rules!" What they mean is that a writer should be free to go where he pleases without feeling hemmed in—and that's certainly true. But you know what? Here's a "rule" you should follow: Establish a POV character readers care about from the beginning. If I was browsing in a bookstore and cracked open the previously described book and read the first couple of pages, I would never have plunked down $24.99 for it. Or $10.99. Or even $3.99. I might have taken it home from the remainder shelf for $2.99. That's called *consumer behavior*. (I actually bought the book for under a buck at a used bookstore.)

Likewise, the "rule" that you ought to be unfolding a story in three acts—because that's how we are wired or trained to receive drama—should be ignored at your peril. This book dragged so much in the first third that I just gave up. (I have since tried twice more to get into this novel.)

How about the "rule" that you should have conflict, tension, and present-moment action in every scene? The long bouts of narrative summary in this book violated the über-rule of fiction: Don't bore the reader.

Or the "rule" that style should serve story, and not the other way around.

Maybe before a writer embraces the "there are no rules" idea, he ought to at least see what the craft teaches about time-tested methods and techniques. I bet the publisher—and hopefully, the author of my example—wish they had done so before publishing this book.

Learn from Failure

The author has since moved back to more familiar genre grounds. I suspect he's better for at least having attempted to write something beyond his comfort zone. Leonard Bishop, the author of *Dare to Be a Great Writer* (Writer's Digest Books), said, "If you boldly risk writing a novel that might be acclaimed as great, and fail, you could succeed in writing a book that is splendid." In this case, the book was not splendid, but if the writer learns from his bold risk and craft failure, he himself may write many more superb books in his career. And thus, this whole episode will have been to his benefit, and that of his readers.

BOUNCE BACK FROM FAILURE EXERCISES

1. What's a past failure for you, and how did you meet it? Did it demoralize you? Or did you learn from it and come back?
2. "That which does not kill you makes you stronger." Do you agree with Emerson? You should!
3. When you receive negative feedback on a piece of writing, write down everything you can learn from it and forget about the rest. (If the feedback is personal, forget about the person entirely.)
4. Reach for the stars when you write. You may not quite get one, but you won't get a handful of mud either. What is your "stretch goal" for your next project?

WHAT WE CAN LEARN FROM BIG CLUNKY NOVELS

Kings Row was a huge bestseller in 1940 and was turned into a hit movie in 1942. The movie starred Robert Cummings and, in his finest role, Ronald Reagan. The supporting cast is equally impressive: Claude Rains, Ann Sheridan, Charles Coburn, and the unforgettable Maria Ouspenskaya.

After watching the movie I decided to read the book. It has an interesting pedigree. It was the author's first novel, and he was fifty-eight when it came out. Henry Bellamann was a musician, a composer, and an educator. He wrote *Kings Row* (which takes place around 1900) based, in part, on his own hometown. This caused quite a stir, as the citizens, who were still alive from those days, took offense to much of the content.

And what content! This sweeping saga concerns a boy, Parris Mitchell, who grows up in Kings Row and goes on to become one of the first practicing psychiatrists in America. His childhood friend is Drake McHugh. Parris is the sober-minded student. Drake is the wild ladies man. The narrative follows their formative years, their loves, their disasters.

Two very dark and sinister secrets dominate the proceedings. I won't spoil them for you here. I recommend you watch the movie ... and then know that one of the secrets is even darker in the novel. The studio ran up against the censors and thus had to soften it to some degree. I can see why much of the reading public was "shocked" by the novel.

Now, here's the interesting thing. The book is not exactly what I'd call well written. The prose is clunky, the dialogue sodden. Yet I couldn't stop reading, and by the time I was finished, I felt a sense of resonance that only a deeply affecting reading experience can bring.

My question to myself, then, was why, in spite of the deficiencies, did I feel this way?

Before I answer, let me mention another book that had much the same effect on me.

In the early years of the twentieth century, most critics would have named Theodore Dreiser as the great American novelist. He ushered in a new school of urban realism. Here was not a Mark Twain, writing lighthearted fare. Nor a Jack London, with his fast-moving action.

No, Dreiser was our "important," world-class novelist. But you hardly ever hear his name mentioned anymore. He's not taught, except on rare occasions, in college literature classes. This is sad, because Dreiser has much to teach us.

His greatest work is *An American Tragedy* (1925). You can also watch the movie version. *A Place in the Sun* (1951) is a terrific film starring Montgomery Clift and, at her most gorgeous, Elizabeth Taylor.

This novel is also clunky in its prose. In fact, the *New York Times* famously dubbed it "the worst written great book ever." Yet when I finished it, I found myself deeply moved.

Which brings up the same question I had about *Kings Row*. Why do I count each of these novels among my most memorable reading experiences, even though stylistically they fall short?

Here's my attempt at some answers.

Great Themes

Both these books take up the great themes of human existence. Love, evil, sin, fate. These books were not meant to be commercial throwaways. The authors worked years on them. Indeed it was ten years between Dreiser's *The Genius* and his magnum opus.

The main characters are thrust into situations that force them to confront all forms of death: physical, professional, psychological. Clyde Griffiths in *An American Tragedy* is obsessed with ambition and success, and then the lovely Sondra. Only problem: He's impregnated another woman who threatens to spill the beans unless he marries her.

Therein lies the tale.

Parris Mitchell of *Kings Row* is obsessed with human behavior, why people act the way they do, and how he can help them. But his explorations of the mind lead him to dark corners he never could have conceived of growing up. It's a loss of innocence and a confrontation with harsh reality.

Nothing seems "small" in these novels. The authors reach for the thematic skies.

I don't see why any novelist cannot treat a large theme in a book. Even in commercial fare, like a category romance. If you're writing about love, write it for all its worth.

Interior Life of the Characters

Both Dreiser and Bellamann spend a huge portion of their narratives explaining exactly what is going on inside the main characters. We cannot help but identify with the emotional stakes and inner conflicts.

Dreiser is especially explicit when, in omniscient fashion, he describes how Clyde is thinking and feeling at key points. What it came down to was not the style, but Dreiser's uncanny ability to show us human behavior and thought in a way that truly makes us understand not just the character, but ourselves.

These days, the amount of interior time you spend depends on your genre and your own particular style. But take note: When you get readers inside a character's head, they tend to bond with him more. And that makes for a greater reading experience.

Huge Action

And the emotional is balanced with the external. The action is not of the thriller variety, but nevertheless is huge. We're talking about murder, suicide, incest, lust, vengefulness, and, of course, the vagaries of romantic love.

Here is a lesson for character-driven writers. You love rendering the inner life of the characters, but if you don't find a balance between internal and external, the action can be less than compelling. The best literary writers give us action that matters.

Here's my theory about clunky fiction that does both those things. By the time you've traveled with the characters through the narrative, you become, by a wonderful alchemy, totally invested in their fate. Whether the story ends on an upbeat note (as in *Kings Row*) or a tragic one (as in *An American Tragedy*), you are going to be affected in the fashion all writers wish to achieve: The book is going to stay with you long after you finish it.

I do enjoy what Sol Stein calls "transient fiction." I read many books that entertain me wildly, but when they're over, they're over and I'm not tempted to read them again.

Yet I often think about *An American Tragedy*. And likewise *Kings Row*.

THE FIVE LAWS OF THE FICTION READER

Without readers, a writer has no career.

There are other reasons people write, of course. For therapy. For fun. For their family. Out of boredom. Because they're in prison. But most writers write to share their stories with the hope of some financial return.

When asked what kind of writing made the most money, Elmore Leonard replied, "Ransom notes." Outside of that particular genre, professional writers swim in the free enterprise system, which usually involves two parties: seller and buyer.

The writer is the seller, the reader is the buyer. The product is a book. Or a story. And in order for this exchange to work, the buyer must like the product.

In order for this exchange to become a lucrative career, the buyer must *love* the product. There are five specific things a reader is looking for in fiction:

The Reader Wants to be Transported into a Dream

Agents and editors often tell fiction writers that a reader wants an 'emotional experience" from a novel. They also say that readers want to be "entertained."

True, but I don't think those two things go far enough. What a reader really and truly longs for is to be *entranced*. I mean that quite literally. The best reading and movie-going experiences I've ever had have been those where I forgot I was reading or watching, and was just so caught up in the story it was like I was in a dream.

I think of my favorite shows as a kid, *Gumby*. Remember Gumby and Pokey? (If you want to keep your age a secret, don't raise your hand.)

My favorite part of any episode was when Gumby and his horse jumped into a book, got sucked inside, and became part of the story world. I wanted to do that with The Hardy Boys: Jump in and help Frank and Joe solve the mystery.

The point is, when you read, you want to feel like Gumby—like you're inside the story, experiencing it directly.

Hard to do, but who said great writing was easy? Maybe a vanity press or two, but that's it.

When I teach workshops, I often use the metaphor of speed bumps. You drive along on a beautiful stretch of road, looking at the lovely scenery, and you "forget" that you're driving. But if you hit a speed bump, you're taken out of that experience for a moment. Too many of those moments and your drive becomes unpleasant.

One reason we study the craft is to learn to eliminate speed bumps, so the readers can forget they're driving and just enjoy the ride.

The Reader is Always Looking for the Best Entertainment Bang for the Buck

In this, readers are like any other consumer. If they are going to invest discretionary funds in something, they want a good return on that investment. Their judgment is based on expectations and experience. If they have experienced a writer giving them wonderful reading over and over, they will pay a higher price for that writer's next book.

If, on the other hand, a writer is new and untested, the reader wants a sampling at a low price, or even for free. Even then, however, they desire to be just as entertained as if they shelled out ten or twenty bucks for a Harlan Coben or a Debbie Macomber.

That's a challenge all right, and it should be. But here's the good news. If a reader gets something on the cheap and it enraptures them, you are on your way to a career, because of the next law.

If You Surpass Reader Expectations, They Will Reward You by Becoming Fans

Fans are the best thing to have. Fans generate word of mouth. Fans stay with you.

So your goal needs to be not just to meet reader expectations but to surpass them.

How?

By doing everything you can to get better, write better. To do what Red Smith (and *not* Ernest Hemingway) said. You just sit down at the keyboard, open a vein, and bleed.

That's not just romanticized jargon. It's what the best writers do, over and over again.

So what if you don't reach that high standard with your book? No matter. Your book will be better for the trying, and you'll be a better writer, and your next book will be better yet.

Jump on that train and stay on it.

Readers Want to Feel a Connection with Authors They Love

Which in the "old days" meant maybe sending a fan letter and getting a note in return; or going to a book signing and getting a hardcover signed and saying a few words to the author.

Now we have tweets, Facebook, blogs, and e-mail—different ways for readers to feel connected to their favorite writers.

This is really what social media is about. It's *social,* not marketing, media. Do it well and build a community. When you have something to offer, you will have earned the right to do so.

Readers Need Stories, so Supply Their Needs

In fact, we all need stories. Stories are what keep a culture alive. Stories shape us—and the best ones shape us for the better, like *To Kill a Mockingbird* and *The Long Goodbye.* The former is literary, the latter is genre, but it's elevated genre—it has something to say that's deep, and in this era of fifty shades of dreck and dross, there's a crying need for books that elevate the soul. This can be done in any genre, even horror (just ask Dean Koontz or Stephen King).

Obey these five laws! Readers will thank you with a fair exchange of funds.

READER CONNECTION EXERCISES

1. How is your writing entrancing readers into a fictive dream? Can you identify places where the dream may be frustrated? Are you willing to have a good beta reader or editor help you?
2. Come up with three ways your novel will surpass reader expectations. Think about plot, character, scenes that surprise, and dialogue.
3. Reassess your social media presence. How can you be more positive and personal? How can you make your social media following glad to read what you post?

HOW TO GET READERS TO LUST AFTER YOUR BOOK

The word *lust* in our language is usually limited to the sexual arena. But it was not always so. The Greek philosophers used the term *epithumia* to indicate an intense desire that can be directed toward good or ill. Whatever the end, the desire is more than intellectual curiosity. It's a feeling of *I really must have this!*

Which is precisely the feeling you want to induce in readers so they will buy your book. It's not enough to make it look "interesting." You've got to hit them with something that raises their *epithumia* so the blood starts pumping the "buy" message to their head.

At least three essential factors go into raising desire levels in potential customers. They are *excitement, killer copy,* and *grabber sample.*

1. Excitement

If you are not jazzed about your own book *as you write it,* it's going to be that much more difficult to excite a reader. So the first order of business is to make sure you are pumped about your own project.

Writing a book is like a marriage. Your first idea and how charged you are about it is falling in love. Once in, you're married to it, and we all know marriage has its ups and downs. You're not always going to be starry-eyed and ready to sing "In Your Eyes" at the drop of the hat. So you struggle a bit, but you're still dedicated to the marriage. (Editing, of course, is marriage counseling.)

Try not to write any scene until something about it excites you. I brainstorm for the unexpected—in action, dialogue, setting, or new characters. Then I start writing.

2. Killer Copy

Your book description is the next lust inducer. It's like that perfect outfit that accentuates the positive, if you know what I mean. It's Betty Grable's legs. (What would be the analogue for the ladies? Fabio in an open shirt?)

Ahem.

A book's description copy (sometimes called "cover copy," sometimes a "blurb," though I usually reserve that term for someone's endorsement) is the writing that sums up the book in a few lines, increasing the reader's desire to buy. It is crucially important. There are people who have marketing degrees who specialize in this kind of writing.

But you can learn to do it. My formula is three sentences and a tagline.

Three Sentences

Sentence 1: Character name, vocation, initial situation

> Dorothy Gale is a farm girl who dreams of getting out of Kansas to a land far, far away, where she and her dog will be safe from the town busybody Miss Gulch.

Sentence 2: "When" + Doorway of No Return

Note: The Doorway of No Return is my term for the initial turning point that thrusts the Lead into Act II. It's where your Lead is *pushed*, via an event or strong emotion, into the heart of the story. Afterward, they can never go back to their ordinary world.

> When a twister hits the farm, Dorothy is carried away to a land of strange creatures and a wicked witch who wants to kill her.

Sentence 3: "Now" + The Death Stakes

Note: Death can be physical, professional, or psychological (see "A Key to Creating Conflict in Fiction," chapter four).

> Now, with the help of three unlikely friends, Dorothy must find a way to destroy the wicked witch so the great wizard will send her back home.

You may have heard the term "elevator pitch." That's what this is: a short plot outline you can spout on a short elevator ride. You can now expand or revise each sentence as you see fit. Just remember this is the "sizzle" and not the "steak." Don't try to pack everything about your plot into the copy. You want just enough to whet the appetite of the busy browser.

Tagline

Sometimes wrongly called a "logline" (that's a screenwriting term for how scripts are "logged" with a sentence describing the plot), the tagline is more of a teaser. It's what you see on movie posters. You'll recognize some famous taglines:

> In space, no one can hear you scream.
>
> *—Alien*

> Don't go in the water.
>
> *—Jaws*

> Earth. It was fun while it lasted.
>
> *—Armageddon*

> His story will touch you, even though he can't.
>
> *—Edward Scissorhands*

> Reality is a thing of the past.
>
> *—The Matrix*

Coming up with a great tagline is fun, but it takes some work. The best way to go at it is to write a bunch of them. Then choose the best ones and refine, rewrite, refine again. Get some help from friends. Brainstorm. Test your favorites on a few people.

These two exercises are a great thing to do *before you ever write a word of your novel*. Because if you can't nail this much about your idea, and pack it with *epithumia*, it's a pretty fair bet you need to shore up the foundation for the long building project ahead.

Here's the tagline and copy I did for my thriller *Don't Leave Me*:

> *When they came for him it was time to run. When they came for his brother it was time to fight.*

> Chuck Samson needs to heal. A former Navy chaplain who served with a Marine unit in Afghanistan, he's come home to take care of his adult, autistic brother, Stan. But the trauma of Chuck's capture and torture threatens to overtake him. Only the fifth graders he teaches give him reason to hope for the future.

But when an unseen enemy takes aim at Chuck, he finds himself running for his life. And from the cops, who think he's a murderer. A secret buried deep in Chuck's damaged soul may be the one thing that can save him. But can he unearth it?

Now, needing to protect his only brother from becoming collateral damage, Chuck Samson must face the dark fears embedded in his mind and find a way to save Stan ... or die trying.

3. Grabber Sample

The final touch in our lust generator is a great opening. That's the free sample readers will see online, or on the first few pages when browsing in a bookstore (remember those days?).

I advise that any novel begin with a disturbance, and an actual scene. In these days of short attention spans you simply must ...

Squirrel!

See how easy it is to get distracted?

What you want is a character whose ordinary world is being disturbed in some way. It doesn't have to be something big, like gunshots or a car chase. It just has to be something unusual that tells the reader there's something troubling or mysterious going on.

Like in James M. Cain's classic, *The Postman Always Rings Twice*:

They threw me off the hay truck about noon.

Or in Harlan Coben's *Promise Me*:

The missing girl—there had been unceasing news reports, always flashing to that achingly ordinary school portrait of the vanished teen, you know the one, with the rainbow-swirl background, the girl's hair too straight, her smile too self-conscious, then a quick cut to the worried parents on the front lawn, microphones surrounding them, Mom silently tearful, Dad reading a statement with quivering lip—that girl, that *missing* girl, had just walked past Edna Skylar.

May I suggest you visit my blog, Kill Zone (www.killzoneblog. com) and type "First Page" in the search box. You'll see all the critiques we've done over the years. I'm telling you, spend a week studying these and you'll be a sample monster, a grabber virtuoso, a hook hotshot.

READER LUST EXERCISES

1. Step back from your work-in-progress (WIP) for a moment. Pretend you are a busy train commuter who wants only to be entertained on the trip each way. Ask: Would this story's premise grab you?
2. Rework the premise in the three-sentence form above. Test it on some friends. Strengthen it until it's irresistible.
3. Create several taglines. Rework them until you have one that could go on a movie poster. Keep that near you as you write. It will remind you of the heat and heart of your plot.

LET ME ENTERTAIN YOU

Some time ago I was on a plane coming back from New York. Sitting in the window seat was a woman of about sixty. As soon as we were in the air, she took a paperback out of her purse and started to read.

Since one out of every three paperbacks in the world is a book by James Patterson, it was no surprise when I saw his name on the cover.

I took out my Kindle and started reading the complete works of Charles Dickens.

After half an hour or so, I heard a ripping noise. I glanced over and saw the woman tearing off a good chunk of pages from Mr. Patterson's book. She folded these and stuck them in the seat pocket.

And went back to reading.

I said nothing, returning to the travails of Little Dorrit.

Another half hour or so went by, and the woman did the same thing with the next section of the book. I held my Kindle in a protective position.

Time went on, and eventually what I guessed to be about half the book was torn asunder. At some point a flight attendant came down the aisle with a trash bag. The woman gestured to the attendant and placed the pages that had formerly been part of a bound paperback into the bag.

I couldn't resist. "That must be a trashy novel," I said.

She looked at me quizzically, which is a look I'm used to.

"I've never seen someone do that before," I said.

"Oh," she said, "before I go on a trip I pick up a few paperbacks at a garage sale. I don't want to carry them around after I'm finished. And if I'm in the middle of a book I don't want to carry the whole book. I read and tear off pages so I'm left with a smaller book to put in my purse."

"Mr. Patterson might feel ripped off," I said.

She stared.

"Are you enjoying the book?" I said.

"It keeps me occupied," she said.

And isn't that why most people read fiction? To be occupied, transported, distracted, entertained? To have a few hours when they're not worried about jobs, relationships, politics, crime, money, or the kids' report cards?

Thus the term *escapist*. And that is not a bad thing. In fact, it may be essential for survival. Unless we can shut down for a while and let our brains be entertained, we are doomed to walk through the dense fog of existence without so much as a candle.

Of course, there is room for what some call "difficult" fiction, the kind of fiction that tests readers, that requires a certain amount of aerobics of the brain. Every year one or two literary novels break out into huge sales. Others may barely make a dent in the market, but win literary prizes. Publishers and authors would love it if literary fiction in general were more popular. But publishers need to make money. They do it primarily with A-list authors who entertain.

Again, not a bad thing.

"In a world that encompasses so much pain and fear and cruelty, it is noble to provide a few hours of escape, moments of delight and forgetfulness."

—Dean Koontz, *How to Write Best Selling Fiction*
(Writer's Digest Books, 1981)

So what are the elements of entertaining fiction? Here is what I look for—and try to write myself:

- a Lead we absolutely bond with and root for
- a touch of humor
- heart and heat
- death overhanging (physical, psychological, and/or professional)
- vindication of the moral order
- surprise, things we haven't seen before
- twists and turns
- a knockout ending
- a style with a bit of unobtrusive poetry

What would you add? Create your own checklist and keep it close!

KNOW THE RULES BEFORE YOU BREAK THEM

During the summer after my first year of law school, I clerked for the Los Angeles District Attorney's office. Seeing how a case was put together and a trial prepared was a great experience. Even better was sitting in the courtroom at the counsel table, watching real-world defendants, police officers, defense counsel, and prosecutors duke it out in front of a jury.

Rough justice, but most of the time juries got it right.

One case I remember well was a man charged with the attempted murder of his wife. This was a middle-class couple in their forties, who would have seemed, at first glance, to be the very picture of domestic tranquility. Turned out it was a second marriage for both, with no children involved.

The man had taken a .45 caliber handgun and shot his wife once. She survived. The man claimed he had suffered a blackout during which he could not remember getting the gun or firing it. "Diminished capacity" (as it was known in those days) took away the mental requirement of premeditation, and thus it could not be attempted murder.

Or so the defense lawyer argued.

He was quite a piece of work, this lawyer, a small fireplug of a man. I remember he came to court for the first day of trial with bloody dots all over his neck. My surmise is that he wanted to look good for the jury and had shaved with a new razor. Oops.

And then there were his shenanigans, which were right out of a bad *Perry Mason* episode. Cross-examining the wife, he asked if she had slashed some of her husband's clothes with a knife. She denied it. With a dramatic flourish, he reached under the table for a shopping bag and withdrew a tattered shirt. "What about *this*!"

The deputy D.A. objected. Before the judge could rule, the lawyer pulled out some slacks and shouted, "And *this*!"

"Sustained," the judge said.

"And *this*!" Some underwear.

"Sustained!"

I glanced over at the jury at this point and saw a few of them hiding smiles.

And speaking of the wife, she was of course the main witness for the prosecution. Problem: She came off as a cross between Margaret Dumont and Captain Bligh. Seriously, I am sure some of the jurors were starting to think not only "self-defense," but "justifiable homicide."

Then it was time for the defense lawyer to put on his case. The husband took the stand. Most defense lawyers will tell you it's almost always a bad idea to let the defendant testify, but in this case there was nothing else. The only one who could testify about his mental state was the husband.

He talked about his wife's continual emotional abuse, how she'd put him down in public and never say anything good about him. She'd laugh at him when they got home. She'd mock him until he couldn't stand it anymore. And then one night he snapped. He said he couldn't remember anything about getting a gun. He couldn't remember anything at all until after she'd been shot.

I was really into trial tactics and techniques, even as a law student. During a break, the D.D.A.—a very good prosecutor who went on to become a judge and is still on the bench—asked me how I would approach the cross-examination of this fellow.

I said, "His lawyer probably told him you'll come at him with a lot of little questions. Why don't you hit him right between the eyes? Ask him, 'Why did you shoot your wife?'"

Now, as any experienced trial lawyer will tell you, asking a 'Why" question on cross-examination is usually a bad idea. It opens the door for the witness to explain his answer, in his own words.

But in this case I felt the rule could be broken. First, it would capture the attention of the jury right off. Second, if the man answered with any sort of explanation, that explanation would prove he *did* know what he was doing (i.e., had the mental state for murder). Finally, if he denied knowing why he shot her, it would contradict everything he'd just testified to. He'd look like a liar, which is what the prosecutor and I thought he was.

I was therefore delighted when the deputy decided to use my opening question. The courtroom went stone-cold silent, and the man actually trembled on the witness stand. He didn't know what to say. The silence went on ... and on ... finally, he said, he didn't know why.

And with that answer, he was done for. The jury was out only for an hour or so before returning with a verdict of guilty.

Looking back, I was pretty brash to suggest this gambit to an experienced prosecutor. But I had been deeply immersed in the study of trial technique. Several years before law school, I devoured books by famous trial lawyers, which were in my dad's library. I also read my dad's copy of *Goldstein on Trial Technique*. I even attended a seminar put on by Irving Younger, famous for teaching trial lawyers how to succeed in court.

So I was prepared to suggest to the D.D.A. that he break a rule in this instance, but I couldn't have done it had I not known the rules in the first place.

Craft mastery in any subject is a matter of study, observation, and practice. As a writer, the better handle you have on the craft, the better prepared you'll be to break a rule when the time comes. You'll know why you're doing it and whether it's worth the risk to break it.

CRAFT MASTERY EXERCISES

Rate yourself on the strength of your writing in the following areas, ten being an almost impossible to imagine mastery:

Plotting	1	2	3	4	5	6	7	8	9	10
Structure	1	2	3	4	5	6	7	8	9	10
Characters	1	2	3	4	5	6	7	8	9	10
Scenes	1	2	3	4	5	6	7	8	9	10
Dialogue	1	2	3	4	5	6	7	8	9	10
Voice	1	2	3	4	5	6	7	8	9	10
Theme	1	2	3	4	5	6	7	8	9	10

Now make a list of the areas, putting your *weakest* area first:

Develop a self-study program for item one. Buy one or two books that deal with the topic and study them. Gather some novels you've read that handle the area well. Reread those novels taking notes on the authors' techniques.

Write some practice scenes utilizing what you've learned. Apply the techniques to your own writing. Then repeat the procedure with item two and so on, down the list.

Chapter 2

DEVELOP YOUR IDEAS, PREPARE TO WRITE

Before there's a book, there's an idea. Many ideas seem to pop out of nowhere. Good. Write them down and think about them later. But the productive writer is also intentional about creativity, doing things (as Dean Koontz once put it) to "strain out good story ideas from [the] boiling soup of the subconscious mind."

WHEN BRAINSTORMING BECOMES A DROUGHT

A writing friend recently shared with a bunch of fellow scribes that she was seriously stuck on the brainstorming aspect of a new project. She gave me permission to write about it. This author needed to solidify her idea and start writing because she had a thing called a "deadline." But, she said, "the story and the characters are seriously playing hard to get."

"Would love any brainstorming tips and tricks if you have them!" she said. "How do you start building your story and characters? And how do you feel productive and intentional when brainstorming is such a creative, often stubborn—at least for me—process?"

It's a great question. Here is what I wrote to her:

> I wonder if part of the deal is what so many of us have expressed over the years with each new book, that it seems to get "harder." And the reason for that, I believe, is that with each book, you improve your craft and your standards go up. You understand what goes into writing a whole book (all the constituent parts) and think, "Man, I've got to do all that again! And better!" So every idea in the brainstorming

phase gets tested, when it should be a time for getting as many ideas as you can without judgment.

I do the following at the beginning of any project.

- Start a free-form journal for interacting with myself, asking questions, going deeper into why I think I want to write this, and also putting down plot and character ideas as they come. I take several days (at least) for this, writing without stopping, but rereading the journal each day, doing some editing on what I wrote the day before, highlighting the best ideas, and so on.
- At some point I take a stack of 3" x 5" index cards to Starbucks and write down scene ideas. These are random scenes, whatever comes to mind. I might prompt myself by playing the dictionary game—open a dictionary to a random page, pick a noun, and start riffing off that. When I have thirty to forty scenes, I shuffle the deck and pick two cards at random and see if I can develop a connection between the two.
- Finally, I want to be able to express my concept in a three-sentence elevator pitch that is absolutely solid and marketable. As discussed in chapter one, this comes down to a simple pattern. Sentence one is character + vocation + current situation. Sentence two starts with "When" and is the Doorway of No Return—this is what ultimately pushes the Lead into the main plot. Sentence three begins with "Now" and the death stakes. Here's an example based on *The Insider* by Reece Hirsch:

> Will Connelly is an associate at a prestigious San Francisco law firm, handling high-level merger negotiations between computer companies.
>
> When Will celebrates by picking up a Russian woman at a club, he finds himself at the mercy of a ring of small-time Russian mobsters with designs on the top-secret NSA computer chip Will's client is developing.
>
> Now, with the Russian mob, the SEC, and the Department of Justice all after him, Will has to find a way to save his professional

life and his own skin before the wrong people get the technology for mass destruction.

The next phase of the project depends on how you like to approach things: Are you a plotter (one who outlines a story) or pantser (one who works instinctually, without an outline) or something in between? (See "The Perils of Pure Pantsing" in chapter six.)

My own practice is to go immediately to the "mirror moment," as it influences everything else. (See "Reflections on the Mirror Moment," chapter three, for more on this topic.) In a mirror moment, a character, right in the middle of the story, is forced to reflect. This becomes critical to understanding the character's inner need.

Now, I know there are some dedicated pantsers out there for whom any kind of preplanning brings out a case of hives. They just want to start writing, and that's okay ... so long as they realize that they're basically brainstorming the long way round. Some contend that this is the best way to find original story material. I would say it is only *one* way. They will still have to do a lot of editing and a ton of rewriting. The process I've described here is a faster and, to my mind, more efficient way of getting to an original story line that you will be excited to write.

TEN WAYS TO GOOSE THE MUSE

Calliope, the muse of epic poetry and story, is a fickle goddess. She drops in depending on her mood, tickles the imagination, and then takes off to party with Aphrodite. Homer famously called on the muse at the beginning of *The Illiad* and *The Odyssey*, and she deigned to answer the blind poet. But many another author, cold and alone in his garret, has cursed her for not showing up at all.

So what do you do, scribe? Wait around for a visit? Implore Zeus to flex some muscle and order his daughter to your office or Starbucks?

No! You don't have time to waste. You've got books to write. So I suggest you take the initiative and prod the capricious nymph of her scornful lethargy.

How? Play games. Set aside a regular time (at least one half hour per week) just to play. The most important rule of play is the following: *Do not censor yourself in any way.* Leave your editorial mind out of the loop and record the ideas just as they come. Only later, with some distance, do you go back and assess what you have.

Here are ten of my favorite muse-goosing games:

The "What If" Game

This game can be played at any stage of the writing process, but it is especially useful for finding ideas. Train your mind to think in *what if* terms about *everything* you read, watch, or happen to see on the street. I'm always doing that when waiting at a stoplight and looking at people on the corner. *What if she is an assassin? What if he is the deposed president of Venezuela?*

Read the news asking *what if* about every article. *What if Tom Brady is a robot? What if that Montana newlywed who shoved her husband off a cliff eight days into their marriage is a serial husband killer? Or a talk-show host?*

Titles

Make up a cool title, then think about a book to go with it. Sound wacky? It isn't. A title can set your imagination zooming, in search of a story.

Titles can come from a variety of sources: Poetry, quotations, the Bible. Go through a book of quotations, like *Bartlett's,* and jot down interesting phrases. Make a list of several words randomly drawn from the dictionary and combine them. Story ideas will begin bubbling up around you.

The List

Early in his career, Ray Bradbury made a list of nouns that flew out of his subconscious. These became fodder for his stories.

Start your own list. Let your mind comb through the mental pictures of your past and quickly write one- or two-word reminders. I did this once and my own list of over one hundred items includes these:

- **THE DRAPES** (a memory about a pet puppy who tore my mom's new drapes, so she gave him away the next day; I climbed a tree in protest and refused to come down)
- **THE HILL** (that I once accidentally set fire to)
- **THE FIREPLACE** (in front of which we had many a family gathering)

Each of these is the germ of a possible story or novel. They are what resonate from my past. I can take one of these items and brainstorm a whole host of possibilities that come straight from the heart.

See It

Let your imagination play you a movie. Close your eyes. Sit back and "watch." What do you see? If something is interesting, don't try to control it. Give it a nudge if you want to, but try as much as possible to let the pictures do their own thing. Do this for as long as you want.

Hear It

Music is a shortcut to the heart. (Calliope has a sister, Euterpe, goddess of music. Put the whole family to work.)

Listen to music that moves you. Choose from different styles— classical, movie scores, rock, jazz, whatever lights your fuse—and as you listen, close your eyes and see what pictures, scenes, or characters develop.

Stealing from the Best

If Shakespeare could do it, you can too. Steal your plots. Yes, the Bard of Avon rarely came up with an original story. He took old plots and weaved his own particular magic with them.

Listen: This is *not* plagiarism! I once had a well-meaning but misinformed correspondent wax indignant about my tongue-in-cheek use of the word *steal*. In this world we live in, there are only about twenty plots (more or less depending on who you talk to), and they are all public domain. You combine, rework, and reimagine them. You don't lift exact characters and setting.

Cross a Genre

All genres have conventions. We expect certain beats and movements in genre stories. Why not take those expectations and turn them into fresh plots?

It's very easy to take a Western tale, for example, and to set it in outer space. *Star Wars* had many Western themes (remember the bar scene on Tattooine?). Likewise the Sean Connery movie *Outland* is *High Noon* on a Jupiter moon. The feel of Dashiell Hammett's *The Thin Man* characters transferred nicely into the future in Robert A. Heinlein's *The Cat Who Walks Through Walls*. The classic TV series *The Wild, Wild West* was simply James Bond in the Old West—a brilliant flipping of a genre that has become part of popular culture.

When zombies got hot a few years ago, I pitched my agent the idea of a legal thriller series with a zombie as the lawyer-hero. I figured most people think lawyers and zombies are the same anyway. Kensington Publishing Corp. bought it and it became the Mallory Caine series under my pen name, K. Bennett.

Research

James Michener began "writing" a book four or five years in advance. When he "felt something coming on" he would start reading, as many as 150 to 200 books on a subject. He browsed, read, and researched. He kept it all in his head and then, finally, he began to write. All the material gave him plenty of ideas to draw upon.

Today the Internet makes research easier than ever. But don't ignore the classic routes. Books are still here, and you can always find people with specialized knowledge to interview. If your pocketbook permits, it's a good idea to travel to a location and drink it in. Rich veins of material abound.

Obsession

By its nature, an obsession controls the deepest emotions of a character. It pushes the character, prompting her to action. As such, obsession is a great springboard for ideas. What sorts of things obsess people?

- ego
- winning
- looks
- love
- lust
- enemies
- career

Create a character. Give her an obsession. Watch where she runs.

Opening Lines

Dean Koontz wrote *The Voice of the Night* based on an opening line he wrote while just "playing around":

> "You ever killed anything?" Roy asked.

Only after the line was written did Koontz decide Roy would be a boy of fourteen. He then went on to write two pages of dialogue, which opened the book. But it all started with one line that reached out and grabbed him by the throat.

Joseph Heller was famous for using first lines to suggest novels. In desperation one day, needing to start a novel but having no ideas, these opening lines came to Heller:

> In the office in which I work, there are four people of whom I am afraid. Each of these four people is afraid of five people.

These two lines immediately suggested what Heller calls "a whole explosion of possibilities and choices." The result was his novel *Something Happened*.

The main lesson: Don't let the inconsistent Calliope rest on her mythic derriere. She's a muse, after all. This is what she's supposed to do.

DON'T KILL YOUR THRILLS WITH PREMISE IMPLAUSIBILITY

The most important rule for writers to follow is never allow any of your main characters to act like idiots in order to move or wrap up your plot! (See chapter three.)

However, there is another rule that is of equal import. While this topic concerns mainly thrillers, it can be applied to any genre. The overall premise of the thriller must be justified in a way that is a) surprising and yet b) makes perfect sense.

This is not easy. Otherwise everybody would be writing *The Sixth Sense* every time out. Not even M. Night Shyamalan is writing *The Sixth Sense* every time out!

So what can we do to up our chances of getting our novel's ending right?

Think About Your Contractual Obligation

Readers will accept almost any premise at the start. They are willing to suspend their disbelief unless, or until, you dash that suspension with preposterousness. In other words, the readers are on your side. They're pulling for you. You have entered, therefore, into an implied contract with them. They suspend disbelief, and you pay that off with a great ending.

I often hear writers say things like, "Oh, I've got a great premise. I don't know how it's going to end, but it will have to end sometime. And if I don't know how it's going to end, then surely the readers won't guess!"

That is called, in philosophical discourse, a non sequitur (meaning, "it does not follow"). I can name one big-name author whose last book was excoriated by readers because it had a great setup and hundreds of pages of suspense, followed by an ending that was absolutely ridiculous. I won't name said author because I believe in the fellowship, and I know how hard this writing stuff is to pull off.

Nevertheless, I've heard said writer say (he/she/it) does not worry about how something's going to end until (he/she/it) gets there. And said author has paid the price for it.

Build the Opponent's "Ladder"

A thriller, mystery, or any book that majors in suspense does not begin with the hook, the body, or the lead character's introduction. In your story world, it always begins in the past with the opponent's scheme. (Note: This is not where you *begin* your book. It's what you, the author, *should know* before your book begins.)

Erle Stanley Gardner plotted his mysteries with what he called "The Murderer's Ladder." It starts with the bottom rung and runs up to the top. There are ten rungs:

10. Eliminating overlooked clues and loose threads
9. The false suspect
8. The cover-up
7. The flight
6. The actual killing
5. The first irretrievable step
4. The opportunity
3. The plan
2. The temptation
1. The motivation

So what you need to work out first is the motive for the scheme. This is in the heart and mind of the antagonist. He is then tempted to action, makes a plan, looks for opportunity, etc. When Perry Mason gets on the case, with the help of detective Paul Drake, they look for clues along the rungs of the ladder, the place where the villain might have made a mistake.

The point of all this is that when you build your own ladder for the villain, it will not only help your premise make sense, it will give you all sorts of ideas for plot twists and red herrings.

Write the Opponent's Closing Argument

This is an exercise I give in my writing workshops. It's simple yet powerful. At some point in your plotting, whether you are an outliner or a pantser, you should pause and put your antagonist character in a courtroom. He is representing himself before a jury and must now give a closing argument that attempts to justify why he did what he did.

This step helps to round out your opponent, giving him added dimensions and perhaps even a touch of sympathy. It also keeps you from creating the dreaded moustache-twirling villain. No stereotypes, please.

I see a pantser in the back row, raising her hand. "Yes, ma'am?"

"I just can't write that way! I have to discover as I go along!"

"And you know what you'll discover? That you have to force an ending onto all that material you've come up with. So you'll go back and try to change, mix, and match, only to discover there are too many plot elements you can't alter without changing everything else around it, so you'll end up compromising at the end. Sometimes it will work, but even popular writers who do it this way only bat around .400 on their endings.

If you follow those three steps, your pantsing writer's mind will still be able to play, but it will play with a purpose."

"But ... but ..."

"But me no *buts!* This isn't easy, you know. If it was, celebrities wouldn't hire ghostwriters when they try to cash in on the thriller market!"

Make sense? Have you ever found yourself backed into premise implausibility? Follow these steps, and it won't happen again!

BECOME YOUR OWN MOVIE STUDIO

In the pantheon of prolific writers, one name stands virtually above all the rest. Isaac Asimov was the author of over five hundred books. He wrote science fiction and nonfiction, and books on math, science, the Bible, Shakespeare, and some of the most famous speculative fiction of the twentieth century.

How did he do it?

He had no life.

I say that only partially in jest. Asimov himself admits that writing was so much a part of who he was and what he did that it limited his socializing. Being so prolific, he once wrote, is "hard on one's wife."

He was always writing, he said, even when he wasn't writing. By that he meant his mind was working on the writing, always tossing up ideas, sometimes unbidden.

Now, the idea of working on more than one project at a time may be completely against your DNA as a writer. I've known several writers who say they simply cannot concentrate on more than one book. My feeling is that it's just a matter of habit. That if they gave themselves enough time and practice, they could certainly do it.

I want you to begin by thinking of yourself as an entertainment enterprise, like a movie studio.

There are three things that a good movie company has to do: They have to decide which properties to option, which to develop, and which to green-light. You, to be a prolific and productive writer, should do the same.

You first have to decide what concepts you are going to put into the development process. Spend a half hour to an hour every week on pure creativity. Play games, use writing prompts, and intentionally think up stories. One of the most prolific and successful authors of our time is Dean Koontz. Early in his career he did this kind of thing all the time.

He made up titles. Just titles. Every now and then one of those would trigger a whole story idea in his head, as I've previously mentioned.

He wrote just first lines. Intriguing first lines that popped into his brain. Dozens and dozens of these, until one would grab him and make him wonder what to write next. And that's what he would write next, just to see where it would take him.

Follow Koontz's pattern. Eventually you will have a list of ideas and concepts that you can keep in a file. Every now and then, go over these ideas and determine which ones speak to you, get your juices flowing.

I take the ideas that I want to develop further and put them into another file I call "front burner concepts."

I will spend some time developing these ideas. I might begin a "white-hot document" (i.e., writing as fast as I can), where I do a free-form collection of thoughts and ideas related to the concept. I might start putting down ideas for characters, plot developments, twists and turns. Doing this with a couple of different ideas allows me to have various projects in development just like a movie studio would.

Eventually comes the decision to green-light a project. This is when I get serious about developing a new book, novella, or story.

All of this is subject to change, of course. Just like a look at daily rushes tells a studio boss a film project isn't going well, I could put a project into what they call *turnaround*. Remove the green light and assess it later. My goal is to have two or three green-lit projects going at any one time.

Have a Labor of Love Project Going, Too

The best movie companies try to nurture at least one labor of love along the way. This is a film that is financed not because of hopes of great, big returns, but because somebody in the company just thinks it's worth doing.

A lot of these kinds of films were made in the golden age of the late 1960s and early 1970s. Some of the best American cinema of all time was smaller, personal projects. Films like Francis Ford Coppola's *The Conversation,* Martin Scorsese's *Alice Doesn't Live Here Anymore,* Paul Mazursky's *Bloom in Love,* and Woody Allen's *Annie Hall.*

These projects started to dry up in the late 1970s, when Hollywood went home-run crazy, always aiming for megahits like *Jaws* and *Star Wars.*

But every now and then another of these personal films will sneak into theaters, catch on, and become reminders of what love can do for labor.

So I advocate that you have one labor of love project in your back pocket. It's a project you can work on with verve and abandon, without a lot of thought about marketing and sales.

Why would you do that if your goal is to make money writing books?

Because a labor-of-love project will *make you a better writer.* The mere act of writing this way loosens you up and stretches your muscles.

In fact, a good practice is to write like wildfire, first thing in the morning, on your love project. Do three hundred, five hundred, or a thousand words on it. You'll find that when you go to work on your main project, you'll be in the zone and you'll have more confidence.

You can even use a journal for this if that's your preference.

Most important, try to write fast, without too much muss or fuss over style. The idea is to loosen your mind and imagination.

SEVEN THINGS THAT WILL DOOM YOUR NOVEL

There are a lot of ways to fail at something.

Like the new boat owner who was filling up his pleasure craft with fuel for that first time out and mistook the tube meant to hold fishing poles for the gas tank. After completing his work he started up the engine.

The gas fumes ignited and blew the boat owner into the sky. He came down in the drink and was rescued, but the boat was a goner (yes, this is a true story).

You can be just as creative in finding ways to avoid writing your novel. In fact, you may be (unintentionally, of course) doing some things right now that will keep you from actually finishing a book—or finishing a book that has a chance to sell.

If you want to make sure you finish (and sell) your novel, here are seven things you'll need to avoid:

1. Waiting for Inspiration

Writers love to go to their favorite writing spot with their laptop or notebook. Perhaps your location of choice is a Starbucks. You sit down with a cup of coffee and hold it with both hands, sipping slowly. Invariably you end up keeping your fingers away from the keyboard. You'll glance out a window, waiting for a skein of geese flying in *V* formation. If no window is available, you'll observe the other patrons and make sure they can see your expression of otherworldly concentration.

You are waiting for inspiration. It must come from on high and fill you like fire.

Until then, you refuse to write a word. If you're tempted to start working without inspiration, you might open up Spider Solitaire immediately. You tell yourself this will relax your mind so inspiration can pour in.

Of course, sitting in a coffee shop to be seen and to wait for inspiration is contrary to what so many writers actually do. They don't wait for inspiration. They go after it, as Jack London said he did, "with a club." They follow the advice of Peter De Vries, who said, "I write when I'm inspired, and I see to it that I'm inspired at nine o'clock every morning."

There's no secret to writing a novel: write, and work through minor problems quickly, then work through major ones after the first draft is completed.

Do things like this:

- **ESTABLISH A WRITING QUOTA.** The quota is based not on how much time you spend thinking about writing, but on how many words you can get down. Consider a daily quota, or a weekly one. Figure out what you can do comfortably and set a quota about 10 percent above that as a goal.
- **REVIEW THE PREVIOUS DAY'S WRITING AND MOVE ON.** By looking at what you wrote the day before, you can get back into the flow of your story. Fix little things, spelling and style mostly, but then get on with the day's work.

2. Looking Over Your Shoulder

The great pitcher Satchel Paige said, "Don't look back. Something may be gaining on you."

It's good life advice, and you should apply it to your writing.

If you want to fail, constantly worry about how bad your book might turn out to be. Pause every thousand words or so and think,

This is about the worst piece of crud known to man. Where did I put the bourbon?

This is sometimes known as the "inner critic," and constantly looking over your shoulder will feed him.

If you think about those doubts long enough, they can even develop into fears. Jack Bickham, a novelist who was even better known for his books on the craft, put it this way:

> All of us are scared: of looking dumb, of running out of ideas, of never selling our copy, of not getting noticed.
>
> We fiction writers make a business of being scared, and not just of looking dumb. Some of these fears may never go away, and we may just have to learn to live with them.

Most writers learn not only to live with doubt and fear, but to defeat them. How do they do that? Mostly, they simply pound away at the keyboard.

They concentrate on the words in front of them and kick that inner critic to the curb.

They train themselves to do this via writing exercises:

- **THE FIVE-MINUTE NONSTOP.** Write for five minutes, first thing in the morning if possible, without stopping to think about what you're writing. No correcting. Just write.
- **THE PAGE-LONG SENTENCE.** Choose something to describe (a room or a character) and write a page-long sentence about it, not pausing to edit and instead going on whatever tangents are presented.
- **THE LIST MAKER.** Whenever you're stuck for an idea to pursue, make a list. Brainstorm ideas without assessing them. Turn off your filter. Get lots of ideas, then pick the best one.
- **SILENCING THE CRITIC.** Writers who have dulled the inner critic don't worry about getting the words right. They get the words written.

3. Ignoring the Craft

Ignoring the craft applies to whether you finish your first draft or not. It's the cry of the artistic rebel who will go to the grave denouncing rules, techniques, and anything that gets within a hundred yards of structure.

This does create a very good feeling, like you're the king of the world. You can completely ignore all of the storytellers who came before you (be sure to call them hacks or sellouts). But the fact is that in doing so, you'll most likely fail to place your book anywhere.

Writers who sell their books and build readerships take the craft of writing seriously. They study it without apology. They have people give them feedback—editors, critique groups, trusted and objective friends—and they read countless novels and examine what's going on in them.

They analyze successful stories. They ask questions when reading and use their findings to help strengthen their work. For example:

- How does the writer make me want to turn the page?
- Why am I drawn to the lead character?
- When are the stakes raised?
- How does the writer integrate minor characters?
- What makes a scene work?
- What's the key to conflict?
- How does the writer handle dialogue?

These studious writers will be spotted reading *Writer's Digest* and books on writing. They apply and practice what they learn, and through the wonder of trial and error find themselves growing as writers.

4. Keeping a Chip on Your Shoulder

Here's a surefire way not only to create a novel not worth reading, but to scuttle your career as well. Decide that arrogance and defiance are your two weapons of choice to bulldog your way to publication.

When you have a manuscript rejected, do not treat it as a personal insult. Don't think of editors and agents as nasty creatures who love saying no, who sit at their computers laughing *Bwa-hahahahahaha* as they fire off their favorite thing: the impersonal form letter.

And definitely do not carry all this to your social media sites and publicly rebuke. By name.

Those who break through and obtain a career believe that they can recover—even learn—from rejection and use it as motivation to write better.

Remember the admonition of writer Ron Goulart: "Never assume that a rejection of your stuff is also a rejection of you as a person. Unless it's accompanied by a punch in the nose."

Yes, recognize that rejection hurts. But it's part of the process and always will be. Remember to do the following:

- **WALLOW, THEN WRITE.** Let the rejection hurt for half an hour or so, then get back to the keyboard.
- **LEARN FROM THE CRITIQUE.** Go through the letter and your manuscript and attempt to draw out any lesson the rejection brings. Understand that people in the publishing industry actually want to find new authors.

5. Writing for the Market Only

Now let's talk about one of the biggest mistakes a novelist can make: chasing the market. You might be tempted to study the best-seller lists, try to identify a trend, and jump on it.

There's a saying in publishing that the moment you spot a trend, it's too late to join. By the time you finish writing something you think will be popular, because it's popular now, that ship will have largely sailed.

Follow the advice of that saying and experiment with something new, something agents and editors look for: a fresh voice.

Writers need to be market conscious. Know that publishers are in this business to make money; they need a return on their investment in a new writer.

But good writers still manage to bring something new to the table, namely their own heart and passion filtered through a craft that enables readers to share their vision.

Yes, vision. Every genre needs it. As superagent Donald Maass says in *The Fire in Fiction*: "What the hell are you trying to say to me?"

To develop a fresh voice try this:

- **EXPLORE ALL FACETS OF A STORY.** Concentrate on feeling the story as well as writing it.
- **READ A WIDE VARIETY OF MATERIAL.** Read outside your genre—even poetry!—not to find out what's hot, but to expand your stylistic range.

6. Taking Shortcuts

Even with the boom in e-books and the ease with which anything can be "published," writers should avoid taking the easy way out when trying to publish. Not everything you write is worth putting out as a self-released e-book.

Falling back on self-publishing for anything you write removes the kind of pressure that you need to succeed. Combining this ease with the chip-on-your-shoulder attitude will create a horrific double whammy.

Your goal should be to build a strong foundation in the nontraditional realm of digital and independent publishing—to find surefire ways to vet your work:

- **USE TEST OR BETA READERS.** Don't trust yourself in all ways. Know that you need objective readers, so cultivate people you trust to tell you specifically what's not working. Then figure out a way to fix it.

- **HIRE A GOOD FREELANCE EDITOR.** Know that the big benefit of a traditional publisher is professional editing, so it's worth it to find a reputable freelance editor to go over your work. Note the word *reputable*. There are less-than-savory services out there that will gladly take a writer's money for very low-quality work.

7. Quitting

If all else fails, and you still find yourself struggling, just remember this: Never stop writing.

Remember the examples of those who persevered and eventually found an agent or got published, like Kathryn Stockett. She wrote and edited *The Help* over a five-year period, then got three-and-a-half years' worth of rejections from agents—sixty in all. It was agent sixty-one who took her on, and the rest you know well.

Published authors will tell you it's all about perseverance—the one characteristic all successful writers share. They'll tell you as long as you've got a computer and keyboard, or pen and paper, you can write. And as long as you write, you have a chance to get published.

Author David Eddings said, "Keep working. Keep trying. Keep believing. You still might not make it, but at least you gave it your best shot. If you don't have calluses on your soul, this isn't for you. Take up knitting instead."

BALONEY ADVICE WRITERS SHOULD IGNORE

Some time ago I cheekily posted on my group blog, Kill Zone, the three rules for writing a novel. The post produced a spirited discussion on what is a "rule" and what is a "principle," but by and large there was agreement that these three factors are essential to novels that sell. The rules are as follows:

1. Don't bore the reader.
2. Put characters in crisis.
3. Write with heart.

Here I'd like to discuss some writing advice writers would do well to *ignore*.

Where does such advice come from? I have a theory that there is a mad scientist in Schenectady, New York, who cooks up writing advice memes and converts them to an invisible and odorless gas. He then secretly arranges for this gas to seep into critique groups across the land, infecting the members, who then begin to dispense the pernicious doctrine as if it were holy writ.

I now offer the antidote to the gas.

Don't Start with the Weather

VERDICT: BALONEY

This meme may have started with Elmore Leonard, who once dashed off a list of "rules" that have become like sacred script for writers. If his advice were, "Don't open a book with static, flat descriptions," I would absolutely agree.

But here is why the rule, as stated, is baloney: Weather can add dimension and tone to the opening disturbance. If you use it in that fashion, weaving it into action, it's a fine way to begin.

Look at the opening of *Bleak House* by Dickens. Or the short story "All That You Love Will Be Carried Away" by Stephen King. Or the quieter beginning of Anne Lamott's *Blue Shoe*. All of them use weather to great effect. Here's a Western, *Hangman's Territory*, from Jack Bickham:

> The late spring storm was breaking. To the east, boiling blue-gray clouds moved on, raging toward Fort Gibson. To the west, the sun peered cautiously through a last veil of rain, slanting under the

shelf of clouds and making the air a strange, silent bright yellow. The intense, muggy heat of the day had been broken, and now the early evening was cool and damp, and frogs had magically appeared everywhere in the red gumbo of the Indian Nations.

Eck Jackson threw back the heavy canvas under which he had been waiting. His boots sank into the red mud as he clambered out of his shelter between two rocks and peered at the sky.

If you think of weather as *interacting* with the character's mood and emotions, you're just fine to start with it.

Don't Start with Dialogue

VERDICT: BALONEY

Starting with dialogue creates instant conflict, which is what most unpublished manuscripts lack on the first pages. Sometimes this rule is stated as "Don't start with *unattributed* dialogue." Double baloney on rye with mustard. Here's why: Readers have imaginations that are patient and malleable. If they are hooked by dialogue, they will wait several lines before they find who's talking and lose *absolutely nothing in the process.*

Examples:

"TOM!"
No answer.
"TOM!"
No answer.
"What's gone with that boy, I wonder? You TOM!"
No answer.
The old lady pulled her spectacles down and looked over them about the room ...
—Mark Twain, *The Adventures of Tom Sawyer*

"Any thoughts that you'd like to start with?"
"Thoughts on what?"
"Well, on anything. On the incident."
"On the incident? Yes, I have some thoughts."

She waited but he did not continue. He had decided before he even got to Chinatown that this would be the way he would be.

—Michael Connelly, *The Last Coyote*

"Name?"

"Robert Travis."

"Occupation?"

"Mining engineer."

"Place of residence?"

"Seventh Base, Jovian Development Unit, Ganymede."

"Reason for visiting Luna?"

"I'm checking on performance of the new Dahlmeyer units in the Mare Nublum fields. We're thinking of adapting them for use in our Trendart field on Ganymede."

"I see ..." The port inspector fumbled through my papers. "Where's your celemental analysis sheet?"

—Dwight V. Swain, *The Transposed Man*

No Backstory in the First Fifty Pages

VERDICT: SPAM (a step up from baloney)

If backstory is defined as a flashback segment, then this advice has merit. Readers will wait a long time for backstory information if something compelling is happening in front of them. But if you stop the forward momentum of your opening with a longish flashback, you've dropped the narrative ball.

However, when backstory refers to bits of a character's history, then this advice is unsound. Backstory bits are actually *essential* for bonding us with a character. If we don't know anything about the characters in conflict, we are less involved in their trouble. (Read Koontz and King, who weave backstory masterfully into their opening pages.)

I've given writing students a simple guideline: three sentences of backstory in the first ten pages. You may use them together or space them apart. Then three *paragraphs* of backstory in the next ten pages, together or apart. (See "How to Handle Exposition and Backstory," chapter four.)

I've seen this work wonders for beginning manuscripts.

Write What You Know

VERDICT: BALONEY

Sounder advice is this: Write who you are. Write what you love. Write what you *need* to know.

Don't Ever Follow Any Writing Advice

VERDICT: STINKY BALONEY

A few literary savants out there may be able to do this thing naturally, without thinking about technique or craft, and those three people can form their own group and meet for martinis.

Every other writer can benefit from time spent studying the craft. I've heard some writers say they don't want to do that for fear of stifling the purity of their work. Some of them get a contract and their books come out in a nice edition that sells five hundred copies. And then the author gets bitter and starts appearing at writers conferences raging how there is no such thing as structure and writers have wasted their money attending the conference—that they all should just go home and write. (This has actually happened on several occasions that I know of.)

Here is some advice: Don't be that kind of writer.

CREATE A COMPELLING CONCEPT

I was going through some old files the other day and came across this little scrap of paper from several years ago. I remember it well. I was on a trip to talk with my publishing house at the time,

Zondervan. I was preparing the pitch for my next project, and as I always try to do, wanted to get it into pristine form.

I had an idea that had been chugging around my brain for a while. It was based on two things: First, an uncomfortable encounter with someone from my past who was insistent on edging back into my life. Second, the plot of one of my favorite novels, *The Executioners* by John D. MacDonald (basis of the *Cape Fear* films).

I put those two items together. This is a great method of coming up with plot ideas, by the way. Dean Koontz has been a master at this. For instance, *Midnight*, one of his best thrillers, is a cross between *Invasion of the Body Snatchers* and *The Island of Dr. Moreau*. Koontz even references those titles in the book itself, to "wink" at the readers who recognize the plotlines! But all the characters and the setting are new, original creations. That's how it's done.

Anyway, I was in the hotel room in Grand Rapids and jotted down this note:

> How far will a man go to protect his family? For lawyer Sam Trask, it's farther than he ever thought possible. Because when an unwelcome presence from his past comes calling, bent on the destruction of his family, Sam must leave the civilized corners of the law and journey into the heart of darkness.

Not bad for an on-the-spot jot on a Holiday Inn notepad. The concept was the basis of my novel *No Legal Grounds* (2007), which became a bestseller and is still one of my favorite thrillers.

The reason: concept. If you don't make your concept solid and simple from the start, you're likely to wander around in soggy bogs and down random rabbit trails. You should be able to articulate your concept in a couple of lines.

> A self-centered Southern belle is forced to fight for her home during and after the Civil War, even as she fights off the charms of a handsome rogue who looks almost exactly like Clark Gable.
>
> To get back home, a Kansas farm girl has to kill a wicked witch in a land full of Munchkins and flying monkeys. Aided by a scarecrow,

a tin man and a lion with issues, she faces dangers aplenty along a yellow brick road.

A simple summary like this is your anchor, your floodlight in the darkness. It will keep you focused and writing scenes with organic unity.

In real estate, it's location, location, location.

In fiction, it's concept, concept, concept.

Make sure you know yours before you start writing.

HOW TO WRITE A NOVEL READERS WON'T PUT DOWN

A friend alerted me to an interesting infographic posted on Goodreads.[1] The subject: Why readers abandon a book they've started. Among the reasons listed you'll find:

- weak writing
- a ridiculous plot
- an unlikable main character

But the number one reason by far was *slow, boring.*

Makes sense, doesn't it? With all due respect to Somerset Maugham, I believe there is at least one "rule" for writing a novel, and that is *Don't bore the reader!*

So if I may channel my favorite commercial character, The Most Interesting Man in the World, I would say to you:

Find out the things readers don't like, then ... don't do those things.

Thank you.

Let's have a look.

Weak Writing

This probably refers to pedestrian or vanilla-sounding prose. Unremarkable. Without what John D. MacDonald called "unobtrusive

---

1 http://www.goodreads.com/blog/show/424-what-makes-you-put-down-a-book

poetry." You have to have a little style, or what agents and editors refer to as "voice." To help you develop voice, try reading outside your genre. Or read poetry, as Ray Bradbury counseled. In other words, get some good wordsmithery into your head. This will expand your style almost automatically.

Ridiculous Plot

Thriller writers are especially prone to this. I remember picking up a thriller that starts off with some soldiers breaking into a guy's house. He's startled! What's going on? Jackboots! In his house! Why? Because, it turns out, the captain wants him for some sort of secret meeting. But I thought, why send a crack team of trained soldiers to bust into one man's suburban home and scare the living daylights out of him? Especially when they know he's no threat to anyone. No weapons. No reason to think he'd resist. And why wake up the entire neighborhood (a plot point conveniently ignored)? Why not simply have a couple of uniforms politely knock on the door and ask the guy to come with them? The only reason I could think of was that the author wanted to start off with a big, cinematic, heart-pounding opening. But the thrills made no sense. I put the book down.

Every plot needs to have some thread of plausibility. (See chapter one for avoiding implausibility in your premise.) The more outrageous it is, the harder you have to work to justify it. Leaving plot points ignored or creating something that's implausible will only pull your reader out of the story. So get to work.

Unlikable Main Character

The trick to writing about a character who is, by and large, unlikable (i.e., does things we generally don't approve of) is to give the reader a *characteristic* that is likable. Scarlett O'Hara, for example, has grit and determination. Sherlock Holmes is arrogant, but has a right to be—he's always the smartest one in the room.

Then give readers at least one reason to hope the character might be redeemed at the end. Ebenezer Scrooge displays a heart when he sees his younger self, and then old Fezziwigg. Maybe that heart can be realized again!

Slow, Boring

The biggie. There is way too much to talk about here. I once ran a three-day intensive workshop all based on what I call "Hitchcock's Axiom." When asked what makes a compelling story, Hitchcock said that it is "life, with the dull parts taken out."

If I was forced to put general principles in the form of a telegram, I'd probably say:

> Create a compelling character and put him in a "death match" with an opponent (the death being physical, professional, or psychological) and only write scenes that in some way reflect or impact that battle.

The principle is simple and straightforward. Learning how to do it takes time, practice, and study, which should never stop.

Chapter 3

WRITE MEMORABLE CHARACTERS

'A novelist," wrote E.L. Doctorow, "is a person who lives in other people's skins." Yes, and the master novelist is one who is able to render those characters in such a way that readers *bond* with them. Without some sort of connection to character, it won't be long before readers set a story aside and move on to the next one in their stack. Thus the most valuable tools in your set are those that create living, breathing, memorable characters.

TOP TEN THINGS YOU NEED TO KNOW ABOUT CHARACTERS

Characters Are How Readers Connect to Story

I've read books about the history of eras, and while interesting, they are nothing compared to a good biography (at the time of writing this book, I'm reading H.W. Brands' biography of Andrew Jackson). Why? Because I am more fascinated with people than epochs. (I once heard history described as "biography on a time line.") I think that's true for most of us.

We all love twisting, turning plots, chases, love, hate, fights, free falls—all of that—but unless readers connect to character first, none of it matters.

On the Other Hand, Character Without Plot is a Blob of Glup

Contrary to what some believe, a novel is not "all about character." To prove the point, let's think about Scarlett O'Hara. Do you want four hundred pages of Scarlett sitting on her front porch, flirting? Going to parties and throwing hissy fits? I didn't think so. What is it about *Gone with the Wind* that makes us keep watching Scarlett? A little thing called the Civil War.

A novel is not a story until a character is forced to show strength of will against the complications of plot. Plot brings out true character. It rips off the mask, and that's what readers really want to see.

"Blob of glup," by the way, is a term I remember from my mom reading me *The 13 Clocks* by James Thurber. I always thought it quite descriptive.

Lead Characters Don't Have to Be Morally Good, Just Good at Something

Two of the most popular books in our language are about negative characters. I define a negative character as one who is doing things that the community (theirs, and ours) do not approve of, that harm other people. *A Christmas Carol* has Scrooge, and *Gone with the Wind* has Scarlett. Why would a reader want to follow them?

Two reasons: They want to see them redeemed, or they want to see them get their "just desserts."

The trick to rendering a successful negative lead is to show, early in the story, a capacity for change. When Scrooge is taken back to his boyhood, we see for the first time, that he once displayed some compassionate emotion. Maybe he's not a lost cause after all!

You can also show that the negative character has strength, which could be an asset if put to good use. Scarlett has grit and determination (fueled by her selfishness) and just dang well gets things done. We admire that, and we hope that by the end of the book she'll turn her determination into something that actually helps those in her world. She does, but by then it's too late. Rhett just doesn't give a damn.

Characters Need Backstory Before Readers Do

Yes, you have to know your character's biography, or at least some crucial events. One question I like to ask is what happened to the character at sixteen? That's a pivotal, shaping year (unless your character actually is sixteen, in which case I'd go to age eight).

But you don't have to reveal all the key information to readers up front. In fact, it's good to withhold it, especially a secret or a wound. Show the character behaving in a way that *hints at* something from the past. Why does Rick in *Casablanca* stick his neck out for nobody? Why does he play chess alone? Why doesn't he protect Ugarte? Why doesn't he love Paris? We see him act in accord with these mysteries and don't get answers until well into the film.

But Readers Want to Know a Little Something About the Character They're Following

Against the advice that you should have absolutely zero backstory in the first fifty pages, I say do what Stephen King, Dean Koontz, Michael Connelly, and almost every best-selling novelist does: Sprinkle in bits of backstory in the opening pages. But only what is necessary to help readers bond to character.

Memorable Characters Create Crosscurrents of Emotion in the Reader

We all know about inner conflict. A character is unsure about what he's going to do, and there's an argument in his heart and soul that gives him reasons both for and against the action. That's good stuff, and one way to get there is to identify the *fear* a character feels in each scene.

But to create even greater crosscurrents of emotion in the reader, consider having the character do something the absolute reverse of what the reader expects. Crosscurrents occur when readers are not only experiencing the surface emotion of a scene or character, but also other emotions that complicate things by running against the emotion that is primary.

Brainstorm ideas for creating crosscurrents, and you'll often find a great one down the list, beyond your predictability meter. Put that action in. Write it. Have other characters react to it.

When Hannibal Lecter asks Clarice Starling to send her credentials into his cell, he does not merely look it over, nor give her a suspicious glare.

> He tapped the card against his small, white teeth and breathed in its smell.

Those actions begin a unique and unforgettable characterization.

It was E.M. Forster, in *Aspects of the Novel,* who defined "round" (as opposed to "flat") characters as those who are "capable of surprising us in a convincing way."

Great Villains are Justified, at Least to Themselves

The antagonist (or as I like to put it, the opponent) is someone who is dedicated to stopping the lead. It does not have to be a villain, or 'bad guy." It just has to be someone on the other side of one definition of plot: two dogs and one bone.

When you have a bad-guy opponent, don't fall into the trap of painting him in only one color. The pure-evil villain is boring and manipulative, and readers won't fall for it. You're robbing them of a deeper reading experience.

One exercise I give in workshops is the opponent's closing argument. (See "Write the Opponent's Closing Argument" in chapter two.) Pretend the villain has to address a jury and justify his actions. He's not going to argue, "Because I'm just a bad guy. I'm a psycho. I was born this way!" No bad guy thinks he's bad. He thinks he's *right.*

Now make that argument, and do it in a way that makes his case understandable to all of us nonvillains.

Don't Waste Your Minor Characters

One of the biggest mistakes I see new writers make is putting stock characters into minor roles: the burly bartender, wiping glasses behind the bar; the boot-wearing, cowboy-hat-sporting redneck truck driver; the saucy, wisecracking waitress.

Instead, give each minor character something to set him or her apart from the stereotype. Think of:

- going against type (a female truck driver, for example)
- an odd tick or quirk
- a distinct speaking style

A little time spent on spicing up minor characters will provide your audience mounds of reading pleasure.

Great Characters Delight Us

When I ask people to name their favorite books or movies and then ask why they are their favorites, they'll almost always name a character. Any discussion of Stephen King's *Carrie*, for example, always begins with the title character.

The Silence of the Lambs? Two great characters. The absolutely unforgettable Hannibal Lecter, and the insecure but dogged trainee, Clarice Starling. Lecter delights us (because we are all a little twisted) with his wit, deviousness, and dietary habits. Clarice delights us because she's the classic underdog who fights both professional and personal demons.

The Harry Potter series takes it to the limit with a huge cast of characters that makes a multifaceted impression. Half the delight of that series is in the story people and the colors they add to the narrative.

Great Characters Elevate Us

Truly enduring characters end up teaching us something about humanity and, therefore, ourselves. They elevate us. And that is true even if the character is tragic. As Aristotle pointed out long ago, the tragic character creates *catharsis,* a purging of the tragic flaw, thus making us better by subtraction.

On the positive side, I think of Harry Bosch and Atticus Finch, both on a seemingly impossible quest for justice. I'm the better for reading about them, and those are the kinds of books I always read more than once.

On the negative side, I think of the aforementioned Scarlett O'Hara. We are pulling for her to do the right thing, to get with it, to join the community of the good. Then she goes off and marries some other guy she doesn't love and uses him mercilessly. When she finally suffers the consequences of her actions we are duly warned.

MEMORABLE CHARACTERS EXERCISES

1. What one word best describes your main character?
2. Why is that the word you chose? Is it close to your own heart? What does it represent to you?
3. If this was the only character you would be known for, are you ready to go forward with him or her?
4. If you are unsure about your answer to number three, go through the top ten list systematically and add new aspects of character.

CHARACTER TEMPERAMENT

It was Hippocrates who first discerned four basic "types" of human temperament. These he designated as *sanguine, phlegmatic, choleric,* and *melancholic.* The names were derived from the names for bodily fluids (*yuck*), which the Greeks thought influenced behavior.

Today most psychological typing still revolves around the four basic quadrants, though with the advantage of modern data. It works wonders for characters in fiction. To that end, I use these designations:

Type 1: The Favorite

This is the *popular* personality, the one who is typically the "life of the party" and who thrives in social situations: Someone like Scarlett O'Hara in *Gone with the Wind* is a popular.

Type 2: The Warrior

Obviously, as the name implies, this kind of character is a fighter, one who flourishes on the battlefield of trial. *Powerful* is another name for this person, who is goal oriented and strong willed. Conan the Barbarian, the character created by Robert E. Howard, serves as a prime example.

Type 3: The Thinker

Also known as *particular*, this character is detail oriented, schedule conscious, and good at seeing problems through to conclusion. He or she also likes visuals, such as charts and graphs. Agatha Christie's master detective, Hercule Poirot, fits this profile.

Type 4: The Mediator

This character, also called *peaceful*, is rather low-key, likes to reach solutions agreeably, and tends to draw people together. Think of Dorothy in *The Wizard of Oz*.

Each of these types comes with a set of characteristics. To make matters easy, I have a table all set for you. Play with your characters by passing them through each type. You will find colors and shades you hadn't seen before.

As you orchestrate your characters, be sure they differ in striking ways. Use the table to help you envision fresh conflicts.

Have fun with it. Let your character have a say in his development. When you start getting surprised that's a good thing—the characters are freshening up!

TEMPERAMENT TABLE

	FAVORITE	WARRIOR	THINKER	MEDIATOR
EMOTIONS	Appealing; Life of the party; Talkative, storyteller; Good humor; Cheerful, bubbly; Expressive; Curious; Good onstage; Present moment	Leader; Dynamic; Active; Strong willed; Unemotional; Confident; Persistent; Compulsive	Thoughtful; Deep; Genius prone; Artistic; Sensitive to others; Idealistic	Low-key; Relaxed; Calm, cool; Patient; Quiet, but witty; Sympathetic; Hides emotion
WORK	Volunteers; Energy, enthusiasm	Goal oriented; Organizes well; Insists on production	Schedule oriented; Detail man; Neat and tidy; Likes charts	Competent; Steady; Avoids conflict; Good under pressure
FRIENDS	Makes friends easily; Loves people; Thrives on compliments; Envied by others; Likes spontaneity	Little need for friends; Thinks he's right; Excels in emergencies	Makes friends cautiously; Content to stay in background; Compassionate	Easy to get along with; Inoffensive; Good listener; Dry sense of humor
WEAKNESS	Compulsive talker; Exaggerates; Egotistical; Angers easily	Bossy; Impatient; Quick tempered; Can't relax	Moody; Enjoys being hurt; Off in another world	Unenthusiastic; Indecisive; Shy; Self-righteous

IF YOU HAVE CHARACTER DOSSIER ADDICTION ...

If you are one of those writers who absolutely, positively feels that a complete dossier for characters is necessary *before you start writing*, here's a list of questions and descriptions you should cover that will keep you happily cobbling for as long as you wish.

Name, sex and age:

Temperament type (see Temperament Table):

Height:

Weight:

Eye color:

Hair color:

Unique mannerisms:

Date of birth:

Where did the character grow up? What conditions?

Ethnic background?

Nicknames:

What were her parents like? Are they alive or dead?

What type of schooling did the character have? What course of studies?

What is the character's philosophy of life, in his words?

Current marital condition:

Children?

Current financial condition:

Current living conditions:

Main strength:

Main flaw:

What is unique about this character?

How does this character break stereotype?

What are her hobbies?

Pet peeves:

Favorite movies/books:

Favorite food:

Mode of dress:

How does this character get along with other people (family, friends, neighbors, co-workers, boss)?

What are his opinions on some important matters of the day, if any (abortion, crime, environment, politics, religion, etc.)?

What is this character's "ruling passion"? What, over the course of her life, does she want to be or do more than anything?

Is the character *more* than real life? How? (Story characters must have *more* passion, *more* emotion, *more* trouble, etc.)

What three words best describe the character?

Take each word, above, and brainstorm with them. Write some free-form notes about actions she might take, things she might do.

How does this character fit into the "orchestra"? How is he *different* from the other characters?

What is the character most *afraid* of that might happen? What does she fear in the deepest part of her soul?

How is this character *vulnerable*?

INNER CONFLICT: What are the two conflicting arguments within the character: one *for* his going forward and one *against*?

How will the character grow through this battle? (What will she think about the events of the story after they're over? What will she learn?) Try a summary thought now.

How will the character show *courage*?

What does this character love most in the whole world?

What is she willing to die for, if anything?

Why do you *love* this character?

Who would you *cast* in the role of this character? (Use opposite sex if it helps.)

Close your eyes, and see and hear the character. Then consider the following.

- What *poses* and/or physical movements do you see?
- What is something *surprising* the character does?
- See a stressful event. How does the character react?
- Hear the character *complain* about something. What is it?
- Hear the character *shout* about something. What is it?
- Hear the character *sing*. What is he singing?

DON'T LET YOUR CHARACTERS ACT LIKE IDIOTS

The other day I watched a thriller from several years ago, and I was enjoying it—up until the last act.

You know what I'm talking about. You get wrapped up in a neat premise until, like a soap bubble, it pops at the end through a series of missteps. Take, for example, the following scenario.

The lead character—a smart, good-looking but otherwise nondescript young woman—suddenly becomes a NASCAR-skilled driver and plows her car into a professional assassin who is shooting at her. Then she *slowly* gets out of her car and walks over to the splayed body and ... *leaves him alone ... does not pick up his gun ... does not make sure he's dead or completely incapacitated!* I mean, a smart young woman would have seen a hundred thrillers where the hit man, who is supposed to be dead, suddenly shows up alive!

By not picking up the hit man's gun, the young woman is left completely vulnerable should the main bad guy suddenly appear. Which, wonder of wonders, he does, accompanied by suspense-movie music. He has shocked and surprised our smart young woman and can now kill her instantly. But because over the last fifteen minutes this deadly, perfect-moves-each-time villain has for some reason been transformed into a doofus, our girl gets away. He chases her through a house. He corners her. But he does not finish the job because he spends valuable screen time *talking to the young woman about how he is going to finish the job!* (This is something I call "Overtalkative Bad Guy Syndrome," or OBGS.)

Then the smart, good-looking but otherwise normal young woman discovers her superpower ninja-warrior princess skills. These enable her to do things like head butt the bad guy and toss him down the stairs. Head butt? Really?

There is, for thriller writers (or writers of any genre), no more important *rule* than this (yes, I said it, it's a *rule*, and if you violate this rule you are taken to the craft woodshed and flogged with a wet copy of my book, *Plot and Structure*):

> Never allow any of your main characters to act like idiots or to suddenly develop convenient powers in order to move or wrap up your plot!

Yes, characters can make mistakes. Characters can make a wrong move. Just don't let it be an idiot move. And don't create a deus ex machina.

There's a simple technique you can use to avoid this issue. Before you write any scene, pause for a couple of minutes and ask yourself two questions:

1. What is the Best Possible Move Each Character in the Scene Can Make?

Every character in every scene must have an agenda. Even if it is only—as Vonnegut once said—to get a glass of water. That's how you create conflict in a scene, after all. Then, after noting the agendas, determine the best move each character would make in order to get his way.

2. What is the Best Possible Move Being Made by the Characters "Off Screen"?

Remember, while you are writing a scene about your protagonist, there are other characters, like the bad guy, who are alive and kicking somewhere else. What are *they* doing? How are they advancing their agendas? Answering this question will provide you with some nice plot twists and turns.

HOW SHOULD CHARACTERS CHANGE?

I got an e-mail from a writer who asked the following (used with permission):

> Dear Mr. Bell,
>
> Ok, so I'm big on stupid questions. I just had a thought as I was musing about my latest book. I know the main character has to change. That's a big deal. But what about secondary characters? What about the bad guy? Do the secondary characters change, but less? or something ... And I want the bad guy to go from neutral to really bad ... Does that make sense? Not something I can Google ...

First off, that's not a stupid question at all. In fact, it's a great question with good instincts about the craft. Here are my thoughts on the matter.

The Main Character Can Change in Two Ways

In my book *Write Your Novel From the Middle*, I explain that not all main characters have to change from one state of being to another. That kind of arc is, of course, common in fiction.

For example, Ebenezer Scrooge. He starts out as a misanthrope and ends up a generous, compassionate member of the community. Martin Riggs, the suicidal cop in *Lethal Weapon*, changes from self-destructive loner to close friend of his partner, Roger Murtaugh, and Murtaugh's whole family.

This type of change comes only through the fire of Act II. A life lesson is learned. Why is a lesson learned here? Because Act II is where the struggle with death (physical, professional, or psychological) takes place. It's learn or die!

At the end, the main character is a new person with something of value for the community. As my friend Christopher Vogler (author of *The Writer's Journey*) puts it, the hero returns home with an elixir: He has new wisdom and insight to share with his ordinary world.

Of course, as I also note, the main character can change in the opposite direction. Michael Corleone goes from a loyal American soldier to the soul-deadened Godfather of the Corleone family. That's because in Act II his father is nearly killed by members of another crime family. At the crucial "mirror moment" (see the next section), Michael realizes he's the only one of the three brothers who actually knows how to exact revenge. Thus begins his negative slide.

But that's not always how a character changes. There's another way. That's when the main character retains the same basic nature but grows *stronger* because of the life-and-death challenges of Act II.

An example is Dr. Richard Kimble in *The Fugitive*. He's the same decent man at the end that he was at the beginning. But he had to learn survival skills. He is forced to grow stronger because he was wrongly convicted of murdering his wife. When he escapes from a prison bus, he has to stay alive and out of the law's reach so he can find the real killer.

Marge Gunderson, of *Fargo*, is the same decent, small-town policewoman at the end as she was at the start. But she has to ramp up her skills to bring a vile murderer and a devious scam artist to justice. These are unlike the misdemeanors she's used to!

So consider what kind of change your main character is going through: change of nature, or growing stronger?

Also consider this: A character can resist change. He can be "offered grace" (Flannery O'Connor's term) but turn it down. That's what makes for tragedy.

In Act IV of *Othello*, Emilia, Desdemona's attendant (and, unfortunately, the wife of Iago) pleads Desdemona's innocence to Othello in no uncertain terms. But when she exits, Othello mutters that she is a "subtle whore" and refuses to believe her. He kills his wife instead.

Finally, change can come too late, which is also tragic. Think Scarlett O'Hara in *Gone with the Wind*.

Secondary Character Change

A powerful trope is the change of secondary characters, brought about by the courage and example of the main character.

Here is where *The Fugitive* rises above most action films. The opposition to Richard Kimble is Sam Gerard, the lawman played by Tommy Lee Jones. He makes it clear early on he has only one job: catch Kimble. When Kimble has a gun on him and insists he's innocent, Gerard says, "I don't care!" Because it's not his job to care. At that point Kimble thinks, "Oh, crap" (my interpretation of

Harrison Ford's facial expression) and so he dives off that spillway and goes *kersplash* in the waters below.

But observing this, and Kimble's other behaviors—as well as seeing what a lousy job the Chicago cops did on the original investigation—Gerard does begin to care. In the end, he helps Kimble get the real bad guy.

Another example is Louis, the corrupt French police captain in *Casablanca*. Watching how Rick gradually begins to take sides against the Nazis, Louis finally finds his conscience at the end, letting Rick off the hook for murdering Major Strasser. To the arriving police force Louis says, "Round up the usual suspects." Not only that, Louis walks off with Rick to join the war effort. It is "the beginning of a beautiful friendship."

This kind of change enhances the theme of a story. We like to see justice and honor prevail. When they do, it ought to be powerful enough to inspire secondary characters, too.

Bad Guy Going from Neutral to Worse

There is no reason you can't show a villain growing more villainous as the story moves along. You can show this via a parallel plotline from the villain's POV, or you can make it the "shadow story." (See "The Power of the Shadow Story," chapter four.) What happens offscreen with the villain? How is he altering his plans, ignoring his conscience, falling further and further from his humanity? Give it some thought and weave that material into the narrative as you see fit.

A plot is about a character who uses strength of will against the forces of death—be that death physical, professional, or psychological. No one goes through such a crucible without changing or becoming stronger.

It's your job to show the change and make readers glad they stuck around for a whole book to see it.

> ### CHARACTER CHANGE EXERCISES
>
> 1. Think about your main character at the end of your project. Interview her as an investigative reporter.
> 2. Ask: How have you changed? Don't accept the first answer. Make the character go deeper.
> 3. Ask: How would the characters who know you best say you have changed?
> 4. Interview the other main characters. Ask: how has the main character in this book affected you?
> 5. Incorporate these changes into your manuscript.

REFLECTIONS ON THE MIRROR MOMENT

In my book *Write Your Novel From the Middle* I describe what I call the "mirror moment." This is a powerful beat I saw happening in the middle of solidly structured movies and novels. (Referenced in the previous section, as well as chapter two.)

In brief, there is a moment in well-structured and memorable stories, right in the middle, where the character is forced to reflect. That reflective moment becomes the real meat of the story. It's what the story is "all about" in terms of character.

There are two kinds of mirror moment:

1. In the first type, the character is forced to reflect and ask questions about his personhood. *Is this who I really am? How did I ever get to be this way? Is this how I'll remain?* In the middle of the novel *Gone with the Wind*, for example, Scarlett has this inner talk with herself. Is she going to be weak or strong? Is she going to be the one to save Tara or not?
2. The other kind of mirror moment is the recognition that the odds are too great, and death is probably inevitable. The character has to figure out how to fight on anyway. In the middle of *The Hunger Games*, Katniss accepts her own death. During this

reflective moment, she decides that the ground she is standing on is *an okay place to die.*

The mirror moment informs everything about the novel, from the pre-story psychology to the final transformation. It's the plumb line. The tent pole. Every scene you write will have an organic connection to it.

Some time ago I received the following e-mail, reprinted with permission:

Hi James,

I own so many of your books, so I want to e-mail you about a small epiphany I had. I recently bought *Write Your Novel from the Middle* and, jaded as I am about writing books, read it with some interest but not much conviction.

Two weeks later, I'm elbows deep in the guts of a novel I wrote seven years ago, and cutting. I mean, I'm slicing and dicing like Freddy Krueger, blood and guts everywhere. I took 20K out of a 127K novel.

And there was that weird passage where my main character has a health crisis (he essentially screws up his immune system from overwork, but he thinks it's something worse) and basically lies flat on his back in his bedroom, waiting to die.

And he realizes that due to the path he's chosen, he's completely alone on the planet, in London, and nobody cares if he lives or dies. It's a moment of great weakness, self-pity, and the existential crisis that propels him—once he gets better—to really work that human interaction, make friends, network. (He's in finance, so being good with people is important.) Long story short, I really gutted the book, cut that scene down by at least half, and some editors said I should cut it entirely, but for me it was weirdly important. It felt powerful, and it wasn't the typical "kill your darlings" kind of vanity on my part. I knew it was important, so I only condensed it and kept it in place.

The book then went to layout. It was exactly 400 pages in PDF.

Guess where that scene fell? Pages 202 and 203. If you take out the front matter/cover, it's SMACK BANG in the middle.

I admit I guffawed.

Thank you for putting your writing advice out there. You definitely blew my mind this time.

The reason I share this is that this writer's reaction is one I continue to experience in my own writing as I utilize the mirror moment and writing from the middle.

Which brings me to Kevin Costner.

Some time back, my wife wanted to watch the thriller *No Way Out* with Costner and Gene Hackman. We hadn't seen it in ages, so I got the DVD from Netflix and popped it in the player.

Halfway in, there's a critical scene involving Hackman and Costner. I paused the DVD. I looked at the timer: We were in the exact middle of the movie.

I turned to my wife and said, "Kevin is about to have his mirror moment." I did not know what it was going to be or how it would be shown. I just felt it was coming.

My wife looked at me the way Jack Palance looks at Alan Ladd in *Shane* when he says, "Prove it."

I started the film up again. And this is what we see next: Kevin Costner staring directly, angrily into a mirror. He has just received information that completely flips his situation on its head. He is caught up in something where there may be "no way out."

I stopped the movie and smiled at my wife.

She said, "Don't let it go to your head."

If you were writing this scene in a novel, you would give us the inner thoughts of the Costner character. He's thinking along the lines of, "This is too much. I'm dead. There's no way out of this ..." That's one of the mirror moment tropes.

Remember, the other kind is a reflection like, *Who am I? What have I become? Is this who I really am?*

An example of the latter is from the movie *Sideways.* This is a buddy-road picture about two friends, Miles and Jack, who go off for a golf and wine trip before Jack is to be married. In the middle of the film they have taken their double date back to one of the girl's homes. Miles, who is insecure and uncertain about everything except wine, opens up to Maya, whose body language is saying, *kiss me.*

Instead of following the signal, Miles excuses himself to use the bathroom. He looks in the mirror, and Miles says to himself, "You're such a ******* loser."

That's what the movie is really all about. Will Miles transform from loser to winner, or at least into someone who is willing to take some chances in life and love?

It's my contention that knowing your book's mirror moment illuminates the entire novel better than any other single technique. And the great thing is you can do this at the beginning, middle, or end of your draft. You can use it whether you're plotting or pantsing your way through.

MIRROR MOMENT EXERCISES

1. Go to the middle of your manuscript and look around. Is there a mirror moment there?
2. If not, ask what main trouble lies in the middle. Is it your character's view of himself? Or is it the fact that the odds heaped against him are too great to survive?
3. In a new file, write at least 250 words of the character's internal thoughts at this moment.
4. Include the best material from this short piece in your manuscript, even if it is only one line.

USING MINOR CHARACTERS FOR SPICE

The poets say, "Variety is the spice of life!"

The writers say, "Minor characters are the spice of stories!"

At least they do if they want their stories to sparkle. And if you want the same, you must spend a good amount of time making your minor characters come alive.

First, we have to answer the following question: Just what is a minor character?

Simple: anyone who is not a major character!

What, then, is a major character?

Simple again: anyone who has a stake in the story and is actively pursuing a goal related to the story question. That means your hero and his opposition.

That leaves us with the minor characters, and we can distinguish between two types: those who are allies or irritants to the major characters, and those who are required to move the story along. Let's take a look at each.

Allies and Irritants

The hero of your story will need some help to attain his goal. He will need people who act as close friends and confidants, or experts in some area or other. There may be a love interest for the hero as well, someone to motivate him to action.

These are allies.

An example of an ally is Han Solo in Star Wars. He is there to help Luke Skywalker. He is therefore a minor character, but since he's given a lot of screen time, Solo could very easily be a major character in another story.

Irritants, on the other hand, get in the hero's way. They may actually be allies of the villain or simply people in the story who make the attainment of the hero's goal more difficult. In the Star Wars trilogy, Jabba the Hutt is a major irritant, though a minor character.

As you can see, allies and irritants can have rather large roles. They are almost always in more than one scene. So it's important that you make them memorable.

Cogs and Wheels

Some characters are crucial to moving the story along. They can be simple or complex, depending on the need. The doorman at the hotel, for example, is simple. He is there only because the hero has to get into the hotel. The doorman does his duty, and that's that.

But what about the cab driver who can't stop talking? The hero is desperately trying to get to the other side of town to stop a nuclear device from going off, and the cab driver wants to drive and chat leisurely about the Jamaican bobsled team. This character obviously has more to do than some other minor characters, and the reader will expect him to have more characteristics, accordingly.

So it is with all your characters. They exist on a sort of story continuum, with stark simplicity on one side and fair complexity on the other. Where they fall depends on what they do in your story.

Bring Them to Life

No matter who your minor characters are, though, you can add pleasure and spice (and everything nice) to your stories by making sure each one is individualized.

How do you do that?

By giving each character tags.

A tag is something the character does or says, something other characters (and the reader, of course) can see. It distinguishes one character from another.

Tags include patterns of speech, dress, physical appearance, mannerisms, tics, eccentricities, and so forth. These set characters apart. And because there are an almost infinite variety of tags, you can make every single one of your characters a unique individual.

Just like life.

Tags will also help you avoid the biggest mistake writers make with characters—writing them as clichés. You know what I mean: the stocky, macho truck driver; the tough-talking waitress; the cigar-chewing New York cabbie; the shy, mousy accountant. I could go on and on.

Don't take the easy route. You can change a tag here and there, even going to the opposite extreme, and come up with a fresh character every time.

You can also decide to give a minor character a trait that adds a different tone to the story. The most common example of this is comic relief. In Star Wars, we're delighted that C3PO and R2D2 are not cliché robots talking in monotone, but unique characters who make us laugh. The former is a fussy valet; the latter is his squealing sidekick. They break the tension of the story and make it richer.

So each time you have to come up with a minor character, ask:

- What is his purpose in the story?
- What tags can I attach to him?
- How can I make each tag unique or memorable?

Let's go back to our doorman. Even a dinky character like that can be more than a cardboard cutout. Perhaps he twirls his whistle like a conductor leading an orchestra. Or maybe he's not a *he* at all—it's a door*woman*, and she gives a little wink to the hero as he passes by.

No matter who the "doorperson" is, he or she will be happy you spent some quality time mulling over the possibilities.

Your readers will be happy, too.

MINOR CHARACTER EXERCISES

1. Create a list of all your minor characters.
2. Next to each name, write something that makes that character absolutely unique. If you don't have something, make it up.
3. Note one way of speaking and one way of acting that other characters would be familiar with.
4. Incorporate these changes in your manuscript.

RAMP UP YOUR CHARACTERS WITH INNER CONFLICT

In chapter nine of my book *Conflict & Suspense* I write about inner conflict. I define it this way:

Think of this interior clash as an argument between two sides, raging inside the character. Like the little angel and the little devil that sit on opposite shoulders in a cartoon, these sides vie for supremacy. For inner conflict to work, however, each side must have some serious juice to it.

I had a chuckle rereading that, which I must now explain.

Some time ago I was in Minneapolis for the annual Story Masters Conference. Donald Maass, Christopher Vogler, and I spent four solid days with a roomful of writers, digging deeply into this craft we all love.

I enjoy Story Masters each year, not just because I get to hang out with Don and Chris and a whole bunch of motivated storytellers, but also because every year I pick up valuable writing information.

That year, during Chris's talk on The Hero's Journey, I was struck by something he said about how we *feel* stories. This came to him, he explained, during his years as a reader for the studios. He noticed that strong emotions hit him physically, at certain points in his body. There were different points for different emotions.

He connected this to the concept of chakra. What happens is that certain emotions immediately fuel a secretion of chemicals in areas of the body. Chris realized that the best scripts, the rare ones that really knocked him out, were hitting him in more than one place.

With a playful gleam in his eye, Chris announced to the class what he calls "Vogler's Rule":

If two or more organs of your body are not secreting fluids, your story is no good.

This got a laugh from the crowd. Thus my reference above to the *serious juice* of inner conflict is apt.

As Chris's session went on, I continued thinking more about this idea. What Chris suggests is that when our "fluid centers" are activated, we are not being rational. Thus a great form of inner conflict, perhaps the best form, occurs when the character's rational mind is assaulted by a strong emotional, er, fluid.

And how human that is! Think of the traveling salesman. He has a wife and children he loves. But at the bar in Wichita he sees a cocktail waitress whose sultry walk and Lauren Bacall-voice unleash inside him an immediate animal lust. The fight is between his mind, which reminds him of all he has at home, and his body, which doesn't care what he thinks at all.

Or what about a sheriff with a high and honorable sense of duty? That's his mind. He's thought this through his whole career, lived by that code. But then killers come after him, and he cannot gather a posse to stop them, and his body starts feeding him fear— of death, of losing the woman he's just married, of being a coward. This is the inner conflict that throbs throughout the entire movie *High Noon*—it's head versus body.

I was reminded of something Iago, who has all the best lines in *Othello,* says to Roderigo:

> If the balance of our lives had not one scale of reason to poise another of sensuality, the blood and baseness of our natures would conduct us to most prepost'rous conclusions. But we have reason to cool our raging motions, our carnal stings, our unbitted lusts.

Shakespeare was describing this very thing, the battle between reason (the mind) and all our bodily "raging motions."

It's such a great way to think about inner conflict, because you can create this tension at any time in your novel. Just arrange for something to strike your character on a strong emotional level, and put that at odds with something he strongly believes.

Thus I came up with "Bell's Corollary to Vogler's Rule" as it relates to inner conflict:

> You must have at least one hot fluid fighting your character's head!

This is where you have so much potential for ratcheting up the readability of your novel. We follow characters not because of what's happening *to* them, but because of what's happening *inside* them. Make it real and full of churning, roiling inner conflict.

INNER CONFLICT EXERCISES

1. Choose any scene in your work in progress. Define the chief emotion felt by the viewpoint character.
2. What is the opposite of that emotion? Write a paragraph where the character feels only that.
3. Justify the emotion. What would cause the character to feel it? What part of his backstory contributed to that emotion? If you don't know what it is, create it.
4. Weave this new emotion into the original scene.

Chapter 4

WRITE YOUR STORY

Want to write a killer story? It starts with a solid structure and understanding of the craft. But you also need help along the way—there are plenty of roadblocks a writer hits on the path to completion of a standout story. Let's remove some of them.

STORY AND STRUCTURE IN LOVE

Some time ago, on my group blog Kill Zone, an author commented about a major obstacle he faced:

> The big challenge … is not taking forever on the prewriting and outlining. How do you impose deadlines on yourself for outlining and still create a solid, damn good novel outline? My fear of drafting a bad story has to a big extent been replaced with the fear of outlining a bad one …

I answered him, in part, this way:

> You've asked a great question. I think it really comes down to fear.
> There's an easier and better way to find story: it's to play *before* you write. Play on the monkey bars built of structural signposts. You actually can be more creative this way because you're not drafting. Thus it's much faster, too.

Try this: Write a free-form document that asks questions about this tale bubbling in your mind. Use questions like this:

- Who are you writing about?
- Why do these characters interest you?
- What sorts of scenes pop into your head?
- What are these scenes telling you about the story?

Write for half an hour or more. Then set it aside and come back to it the next day. Add to it, ask more questions. Burn, baby, burn.

Do this for five straight days and you will have a deep soil full of gold nuggets for your plot.

You can also play in the actual writing. But you'll be playing a game that readers can make sense of.

It's the best of both worlds. Freedom *and* focus, and a lot less frustration. The "best of both worlds" combines the playfulness and creativity of the pantser with the beautiful form of the plotter, all with that most important person in mind—the reader!

If you want to sell books and not just feel good about your writing, you need more than pure freedom and more than mere outlining.

You need a guide, a map, a blueprint—one that is flexible and freeing, not cold and ruthless.

Story *loves* structure, because structure translates story into a form that enables reader connection … and those are the stories that sell.

And don't confuse structure with outlining, which causes pantsers to break out in the cold sweats. This is a common error. Any writer of any temperament can make the most of structure principles, even if your approach is the seat-of-the-pants variety. To be aware of structure is not the same thing as writing a forty-page, single-spaced outline. Which is a perfectly legit thing to do. Just ask James Patterson. Or many fine writers of the past.

When I talk about structure, I mean the storytelling template that seems to be ingrained in us (as human beings), either through nature or due to the way myths and stories have unfolded over the millennia.

Structure is simply beginning, middle, and end. That's three acts. The beginning is the first 20 percent of a novel, and the end is the last 25 percent or so. In between is Act II, where the main plot unfolds.

But outlining is not a requirement. Structure is a good thing for any type of writer because of what I call "signpost scenes." These are key scenes in a well-structured story, scenes you can write toward as you move along. If you know structure, you can anticipate the kind of scene you should *write toward*. Then you can be free in how you write to get there.

For example, I teach signposts called the Opening Disturbance and the Doorway of No Return Number One. The Opening Disturbance is the very beginning of the novel. The Doorway of No Return Number One is the scene that thrusts the protagonist into the crucible of Act II.

You can write the first scene knowing that the next signpost is the Doorway of No Return. And you have room to improvise how you get there.

In 2015, the longtime literary editor for *Playboy*, Alice K. Turner, went to her final review at age seventy-five. Her obituary in the *New York Times* talked about how she championed literary fiction for twenty years, bringing a measure of respectability, ahem, between the folds. And she truly did, publishing some of the best writers of our time and discovering new talent.

I love what she said about her preference for a solid, well-structured plot: "If you're good enough, like Picasso, you can put noses and breasts wherever you like. But first you have to know where they belong."

LET ME TELL YOU ABOUT SHOWING AND TELLING

If there is any bit of advice that is ironclad for fiction writers, it is the axiom "Show, don't tell." Yet confusion about this aspect of the craft is one of the most common failings for beginning writers. If you want your fiction to take off in the reader's mind, you must grasp the difference between showing and telling.

That distinction is simply this. Showing is like watching a scene in a movie. All you have is what is on the screen before you. What the characters *do* or *say* reveals who they are and what they're feeling.

Telling, on the other hand, merely explains what is going on in the scene, or inside the characters. It's like you are recounting the movie to a friend.

Another term used for telling is *narrative summary*. It's where you, the narrator/author, just tell us what happened.

Remember the scene in *Jurassic Park*, where the newcomers catch their first glimpse of a dinosaur? With mouths open and eyes wide, they stand and look at this impossible creature before we, the audience, see it.

All we need to know about their emotions is written on their faces. We are not given a voice in their heads. We know what they are feeling just by watching.

In a story, you would describe it in just that fashion: "Mark's eyes widened and his jaw dropped. He tried to take a breath, but breath did not come. ..." The reader feels the emotions right along with the character.

That is so much better than telling it like this, "Mark was stunned and frightened."

One of the best "show" novels ever written is the classic detective tale *The Maltese Falcon* by Dashiell Hammett. Hammett ushered in a whole new writing style, called "hard boiled," with this book. The mark of that style is that everything occurs just as if it were happening before us on a movie screen (which is one reason this book translated so well into a movie).

In one scene, the hero, Sam Spade, has to comfort the widow of his partner, Miles Archer, who was recently shot to death. She comes rushing into his office, and into his arms. Spade is put off by her crying, because he knows it's mostly phony.

Now, Hammett could have written something like, "The woman threw herself, crying, into Spade's arms. He detested her crying. He detested her. He wanted to get out of there."

That's telling. But look at what the masterful Hammett does:

"Did you send for Miles's brother?" he asked.

"Yes, he came over this morning." The words were blurred by her sobbing and his coat against her mouth.

He grimaced again and bent his head for a surreptitious look at the watch on his wrist. His left arm was around her, the hand on her left shoulder. His cuff was pulled back far enough to leave the watch uncovered. It showed ten-ten.

See how much more effective this is? We *see* Spade glancing at his watch, which tells us just how unsympathetic he is to this display of emotion. It reaches us much more powerfully.

Too Much Telling is Lazy

Here is an example of lazy telling from a best-selling writer. It comes in the second paragraph of the book:

She cared, she loved, she worked hard at whatever she did, she was there for the people who meant something to her, she was artistic in ways that always amazed her friends, she was unconsciously beautiful, and fun to be with.

There are two major problems with this paragraph.

First, it is pure telling and therefore does not advance the character or story at all. Why not? Because we, as readers, are being asked to take the author's word for it rather than having the author do the harder work of showing us the character in action.

Second, it's an exposition dump. There is no *marbling* of the essential information (the way you look at a good rib-eye steak and see the fat marbled into the meat!). It's just poured out all at once and therefore has no effect but dullness.

But You Can't Show Everything

A novel that tried to *show* every single thing would end up totaling a thousand pages or more, most of it boring. The rule is, the more intense the moment, the more showing you do.

Now let's talk about *exposition,* which is explanatory information that a reader *needs* to know in order to understand the story or character. Mark this down as a guiding principle:

> Readers only relate to exposition on a need-to-know basis!

That is, the first thing you want to do is to cut any exposition that is not necessary. By necessary I mean information that deepens the character or explains plot points.

A further tip: Delay as much exposition as you can for the first 10 percent of your novel. If you can create a mystery about it, even better. But understand that the readers will wait a long time before getting answers as long as they are caught up in a solid plot.

When it comes to actual exposition, you may be tempted to put it into narrative form.

> Marsha knew Ted had lost his position after a botched surgery. Obviously he wanted to use her to get another one.

You have two better alternatives.

Dialogue

Exposition can easily come through dialogue—so long as it sounds exactly like what two people would say to each other. Not like this.

> "I know what you're up to Ted, my former family doctor."
>> "But Marsha, we've known each other for ten years, remember? We met just before you got married to Bob, the lawyer you divorced last year."

Instead, make the dialogue *confrontational.* Arguments are especially good for this.

> "Get out, Ted."
>> "Not until you hear me out."
>> "I don't need to hear another word—"
>> "It wasn't my fault!"
>> "A girl died because of your incompetence!"
>> "I was never found guilty by a board of inquiry."

"But you can't practice medicine, can you?"

"I can if I can get some references, if I—"

"Don't come sniffing around here for that."

Internal Dialogue

The other way to do it is via internal thoughts. These should be in the voice of the character.

"Get out, Ted."

"Not until you hear me out."

I don't need to hear about your botched surgery. I don't need to hear about the girl who died.

SHOW, TELL, AND EXPOSITION EXERCISES

1. Find three scenes in your novel where you used narrative exposition.
2. Try converting each instance into a dialogue confrontation. Note: This doesn't have to be a violent argument, just two people in a tense exchange.
3. Now try putting the exposition in the form of a character's thought pattern.
4. Tweak and revise.

HOW TO HANDLE EXPOSITION AND BACKSTORY

Nothing slows down a novel quite like large mounds of exposition and backstory. *Exposition* is material the author puts on the page to explain context. *Backstory* is story material that happened in the past but for some authorial reason is dropped in the present. When this kind of material appears in the middle of a scene it can slow the pace, sort of like a Mastodon trying to escape a hungry caveman by way of the tar pits.

Now, let me be clear that not all exposition and backstory is bad. In fact, properly handled, it's tremendously helpful for bonding reader with character. But if it's plopped down in large doses, and without a strategy in mind, it becomes a pool of hot goo where the story gets pitifully stuck.

Here is how to handle exposition and backstory, especially at the beginning of the story.

First, ask yourself, is it necessary at all? Quite often the writer has all this story info in his head and thinks the reader has to know most of it to understand what's going on. Not so! Readers get into story by way of characters facing a challenge, conflict, change, or trouble. If you give them that, they will wait a *long time* before wanting to know the whys and wherefores.

Second, put a lot of this material in dialogue. Dialogue is your best friend. Make sure there is some form of tension or conflict in the dialogue, even if it is simply one character feeling fearful or nervous. Arguments are especially good for exposition and backstory. Recently I watched the Woody Allen film *Blue Jasmine* and nodded approvingly at an early scene between Augie (Andrew Dice Clay) and his ex-wife, Ginger (Sally Hawkins). They're arguing about Ginger's sister, who calls herself Jasmine. A lot of background is revealed in this exchange:

"What's the rush, Ginger? You got a date?"

"It's none of your business. It happens to be Jeanette, so ..."

"Jeanette?"

"Jasmine."

"What's she doing in town?"

"She's living with me till she gets back on her feet. She's had a bad time."

"When she had money, she wanted nothing to do with you. Now that she's broke, she's moving in."

"She's not just broke. She's screwed up. And it's none of your damn business. She's family."

"She stole our money."

"Okay!"

"Understand? We could have been set. That was our whole chance in life."

"For the last time, Augie, he was the crook, not her, okay? What the hell did she know about finance?"

"Don't stand there and tell me that. She's married to a guy for years, up to his ass in phony real estate and bank fraud. She knew nothing about it? Believe me, she knew, Ginger."

Third: Act first, explain later. Stamp this axiom on your writer's brain. Or put it on a note and tape it where you can see it. This advice never fails.

Let's have a look at the opening of one of Robert B. Parker's Jesse Stone novels, *Stranger in Paradise:*

> Molly Crane stuck her head in the doorway to Jesse's office.
>
> "Man here to see you," she said. "Says his name's Wilson Cromartie."
>
> Jesse looked up. His eyes met Molly's. Neither of them said anything. Then Jesse stood. His gun was in its holster on the file cabinet behind him. He took the gun from the holster and sat back down and put the gun in the top right-hand drawer of his desk and left the drawer open.
>
> "Show him in," Jesse said.

As we will find out, Jesse Stone knows this Cromartie very well. He's called "Crow," and he's a Native American hit man. Lots of backstory lies between Jesse and Crow, but Parker doesn't reveal any of yet.

What he does instead is *show* Jesse getting his gun ready. That's intriguing. He knows something about this man after all, and it requires his gun being ready. Act first, explain later. The scene continues:

> Molly went and in a moment returned with the man.
>
> Jesse nodded his head.
>
> "Crow," he said.
>
> "Jesse Stone," Crow said.
>
> Jesse pointed to a chair. Crow sat. He looked at the file cabinet.
>
> "Empty holster," he said.
>
> "Gun's in my desk drawer," Jesse said.
>
> "And the drawer's open," Crow said.
>
> "Uh-huh."

We now know that this Crow is someone who notices things, especially when it comes to guns. What kind of person is that? We don't know and Parker isn't telling us. We only know this guy is probably dangerous. This is not friendly small talk. The air is crackling with potential trouble.

Half a page later, we get this:

> "Last time I saw you was in a speedboat dashing off with a lot of money," Jesse said.
>
> "Long time back," Crow said. "Longer than the statute of limitations."
>
> "I'd have to check," Jesse said.
>
> "I did," Crow said. "Ten years."
>
> "Not for murder," Jesse said.
>
> "You got no evidence I had anything to do with murder."

Boom. Now we get backstory information, but notice where it is. In dialogue! And that, indeed, is how Parker delivers almost all the essential information in this novel.

Of course, Parker is writing in a particular, stripped-down style. But the principles he uses will serve you as well.

It may be your choice to render some backstory in narrative form. If you do, let me remind you of a rule of thumb (not the same as an unbreakable rule!) that I briefly mentioned earlier, one that I've passed on to many students with good results: In your first ten pages you can have three sentences of backstory, used all at once or spread out. In your second ten pages you can have three *paragraphs* of backstory, used all at once or spread out. But if you put backstory or exposition into dialogue, then you're free to use your own discretion. Just be sure the dialogue is truly what the characters would say and doesn't come off as a none-too-clever info dump.

Writing teachers place a lot of emphasis on sharp, intriguing openings for good reason. Because that's what editors, agents, and browsing readers look at first. We don't want to leave them in the tar pits—we want them to keep on reading!

These tips will help keep you out of the goo.

EXPOSITION AND BACKSTORY EXERCISES

1. Go through your first 5,000 words and highlight all exposition and backstory.
2. Cut this material and save it in another document.
3. Read over the edited words and ask how much of it is *necessary* in these opening pages. Be ruthless in deciding what a reader has to know, as opposed to what you *think* they have to know.
4. Dribble in the necessary material this way:
5. Three sentences worth in the first 2,500 words, either together or all at once.
6. Three paragraphs worth in the next 2,500 words, together or all at once.

THE POWER OF THE SHADOW STORY

I was at a conference once and a new writer came up to me. She said she had a great concept and had used one of my books to outline the plot. She was now 30,000 words into the novel and scared. She said it felt like she was looking out at sea from a tiny raft. There was this *long* way to go in Act II, but now she wasn't sure she had enough plot material to make it.

"Ah," I said like a liposuction surgeon, "the sagging middle. No worries. I'm here to help!"

We sat and talked a bit about signpost scenes, and she understood all that. But it was clear she needed more "story stuff" in her plans.

So I suggested she write the shadow story. This is the part of the novel many writers never think about, yet it's one of the most powerful plotting techniques there is. It will take you places you'd never find if you only danced around in the light.

Simply put, the shadow story is what is taking place away from the scene you are writing. It's what the other characters are doing 'offscreen." By giving thought to the shadows, even minimally, you greatly expand your store of plot material.

A few tips for how to do this successfully follow:

Start with the Antagonist

The most important shadow is the opposition character. Someone once said a good plot is two dogs and one bone. So while your lead is gnawing the bone in one scene, your antagonist (offscreen) is laying plans to snatch that bone away, or setting in motion a scheme to kill the lead dog, or messing with the dogs who are helping the lead dog.

Or maybe he's overusing canine metaphors.

Whatever it is, by getting into the head of the opposition character, who is somewhere else, you will come up with all sorts of ideas for plot complications. It's almost automatic. Fresh scenes, mysteries, obstacles—even new characters—will spring up from your writer's mind. Your Act II problems will begin to melt away.

Do the Same with Supporting Characters

You also have a cast of supporting characters—major and minor—all who have lives, plans, and motives of their own. Here you will find the fodder for those plot twists every reader loves. Like when a seeming ally turns out to be a betrayer. Or an enemy becomes a friend. Why would that happen? Let their shadow stories tell you.

Shadows Inside the Lead

You can also delve into the shadows and secrets of your lead. Maybe you've done this already by giving your lead a backstory and answering key questions about her life (education, hopes, fears, lost loves, etc.).

But every now and then, in the middle of writing, pause to come up with something going on inside the lead that even she is not aware of. Try what I call "the opposite exercise": The lead, in a scene, has a specific want or need (if she doesn't, you need to find one for her fast or cut that scene). Now, pause and ask: What if your lead wanted something the exact opposite of this want or need? What would that be? List some possibilities. Choose one of those. Ask: Why would she want that? How could it mess with her head?

Then look for ways to manifest this inner shadow in some of your scenes.

Or imagine your lead *doing* something that is the opposite of what the reader or, more important, *you* would expect in that scene. What sort of shadow (secret) made her do that?

Just by asking these sorts of questions, you deepen your lead and add interesting crosscurrents to the plot.

That's the power of the shadow story.

Practical Tools

There are two excellent ways to keep track of your shadow story material in your work-in-progress.

One of them is called Scrivener. I know some people are intimidated by all the bells and whistles this program offers. My advice is to start off by using it for just a couple of simple things (mapping your scenes on the corkboard and keeping track of your cast of characters) and then learn other tools at your own pace, only if you want to. At such a reasonable price, Scrivener is cost-effective for whatever you use it for.

In the Inspector View, there's a box labeled "Document Notes." This is place where you can jot down anything relating to the scene on the left. Perfect for shadow story. You can be as brief or as detailed as you like.

The other method is to use the Comments function in Microsoft Word. Just insert a comment, which gives the shadow material.

Remember, all sorts of good stuff happens in the shadows. Go there, snoop around, then come back to the light and finish your novel.

A KEY TO CREATING CONFLICT IN FICTION

One of my favorite movies of all time is *12 Angry Men*, the 1957 film directed by Sidney Lumet and written by Reginald Rose (based on

his play). The plot is disarmingly simple: Twelve jurors deliberate in a capital murder case. The entire drama, save for a short prologue, takes place inside the jury room.

At first, the verdict seems like a done deal. All the early chatter is about how guilty the defendant is (he's a slum kid, accused of stabbing his father). One of the jurors (Jack Warden) has tickets to the ballgame and would love to get out early. Others don't see the point in spending a great deal of time actually deliberating.

They take an initial vote. And only one juror, Number 8 (Henry Fonda), votes "not guilty." Everybody else grumbles.

And for the next hour and a half, we sit in on the deliberations.

The movie violates all the currently fashionable, postmodern, ADHD stylistic conventions. No quick cuts or explosions or overbearing music. It's all talk. It's even in black-and-white, for crying out loud!

Yet, no matter where I happen to come in on the film when it's on television, if I start to watch I have to finish.

Why? Because intercharacter conflict works its magic. What Rose (the writer) did was bring together twelve distinct characters, each with his own background, baggage, and personality, and throw them into what is essentially a great, big argument.

Therein lies the real untapped secret of creating conflict: *orchestration.* That means you cast your characters so they have the potential of conflict *with every other character.*

In *12 Angry Men,* for example, there's a Madison Avenue ad man (Robert Webber) who spouts bromides and tosses out suggestions, just like he would at a brainstorming meeting at the office. 'Let's run it up the flagpole and see if anybody salutes." He's amiable, easy with a laugh. But he never makes a final decision. He vacillates. Finally another juror (Lee J. Cobb) gets fed up. "The boy in the gray flannel suit here is bouncing back and forth like a Ping-Pong ball!"

There's a mousy bank clerk (John Fiedler) who automatically draws satirical comment from the blustering salesman (Warden). There's a coldly rational stockbroker (E.G. Marshall) who arrogantly dismisses all reasonable doubt, until he's backed into a corner by Fonda. There's a young man who grew up in the slums (Jack Klugman) who, at one point, turns to E.G. Marshall and asks, "Pardon me, don't you sweat?"

"No, I don't," Marshall says. There is nothing more to that exchange, but the line is memorable because of Rose's superb orchestration, knowing the personalities and quirks of all his characters.

Then there's the bigot (Ed Begley), who in one unforgettable moment alienates *everyone* else on the jury.

But it is, finally, the main conflict between Cobb and Fonda that is the focus of the drama. Cobb wants to get this kid executed (for reasons that become heartbreakingly clear at the end). Fonda wants to give the kid his due under the Constitution—the requirement of proof beyond a reasonable doubt.

And that's another lesson about conflict: the stakes. They have to be high. In fact, I hold that death must be on the line. Not just physical death, mind you. There is also professional and psychological death. Unless you have one of these overhanging your protagonist, your story is not going to be as gripping as it should be.

In *12 Angry Men*, physical death is on the line for the kid, but more important, it's a matter of psychological death for each of the jurors. After all, they might send an innocent man to the chair. In addition, each of them has some inner baggage to deal with, such as the old man (Joseph Sweeney), whose family ignored him, and the newly naturalized citizen trying to make it in America (George Voskovec).

Orchestration for conflict is essential in any genre, including comedy. *Especially* comedy. Consider the movie *City Slickers*. You have three friends from the city going on a cattle drive out west. They are very different from each other—one is a joker, one is macho, one is laconic. Then they come in contact with someone who is unlike any of them—Curly, the ramrod. The comedy flows naturally out of the conflict between the different personalities.

So as you're getting ready to write, you would do well to take a grid and create a chart of all of your important characters. Then figure out points of conflict between all the characters.

Trouble is your business, my writer friend. Go make some.

CONFLICT EXERCISES

1. Go through your manuscript scene by scene.
2. Ask: Which characters are in conflict, and why?
3. Ramp up the conflict by 10 percent. Add more passion, more emotion.

SUPERCHARGE YOUR NOVEL WITH ONE SIMPLE EXERCISE

In November, writers all over the world jump into National Novel Writing Month, or NaNoWriMo. The goal is to write a 50,000-word novel in one month (an average of 1,666.6667 words a day). It's a blast—a communal expression of the love of writing. And it's a kick in the pants to produce words and not just sit around Starbucks all day talking about writing a novel.

I love the vibe of NaNoWriMo. And over the years I've developed some quick exercises to help writers as they clack away at their keyboards—even if they're not participating in the national exercise.

One of them will prevent you from producing scenes that have no organic connection to the plot, which is the big challenge in this hard-charging contest.

I call this exercise "Because ..."

It has two parts. First, you hone your basic plot into a single sentence. Then, you add a "because" clause which explains what's at stake.

Your plot sentence consists of an adjective, a noun, and a verb clause (the action). Thus:

- *Gone with the Wind* is about a Southern belle who has to fight to save her home during the Civil War.
- *Die Hard* is about a New York cop who has to save a building full of people from a gang of ruthless terrorists.
- *Casablanca* is about an American café owner in French-occupied territory during WWII, who has to battle Nazis and lost love and a corrupt police captain.

Every plot can be rendered in this fashion, and it's important that you know this much about yours.

Once you have your plot sentence, add a "because" sentence that explains what the stakes are. Don't worry about the form of the sentence; just pack reasons the lead character in your novel must succeed into the sentences. Turn it into a paragraph if you want to. It's all for you.

- *Gone With the Wind* is about a southern belle who has to fight to save her home during the Civil War ... because if she loses it, she'll be dependent on others for her existence and will never be a woman of strength or substance.
- *Die Hard* is about a New York cop who has to save a building full of people from a gang of ruthless terrorists ... because if he loses, his ex-wife will die along with the other hostages, and he will have failed in his most essential cop duty, saving people from bad guys.
- *Casablanca* is about an American café owner in French-occupied territory during WWII, who has to battle Nazis and lost love and a corrupt police captain ... because if he loses, the war effort will be harmed (the Nazis will win) and he'll have destroyed the lives of several people around him. And also if he loses, he'll have become a wretched individual with no concern about others, sadly drinking himself to death, having lost whatever ideals he once held.

Believe me, this little exercise is going to pay big dividends for you. When you write, if you start to feel lost, simply go back to this controlling premise and think up fresh scenes for the lead character. Then determine which of those scenes involve him taking steps to solve the main problem.

Let's say we've started writing *Casablanca* and we come to the point where Rick sees Ilsa in his café for the first time. What a great scene we've written! They look at each other, and Rick's heart pounds with a mix of love and hate, desire and the pain of betrayal. Now what?

We brainstorm some scenes. What could happen next?

- Rick punches Ilsa's husband, Victor Laszlo, in the face, and a big fight ensues.
- Rick throws a drink in Ilsa's face, and Laszlo socks Rick.
- Ilsa runs out into the night and Rick chases after her.
- Rick gets drunk and waits for her to show up.

After some reflection, we decide on the last one. This scene gives us an opportunity for Rick to remember what happened in Paris. Then Ilsa comes in. We envision Ilsa falling into Rick's arms ... no, not enough conflict ... how about she tries to explain what happened in Paris and Rick basically calls her a whore ... ooh, that sounds right, because our premise tells us the novel is partly about whether Rick will end up as a wretched human being ...

And so on. In this way you can use this exercise to help build scenes and develop ideas.

THE TWO POWER QUESTIONS EVERY WRITER SHOULD ASK

So you're writing along in your latest novel or novella, and you come to a screeching (or, at least squealing) halt. Your story has stalled. Your characters are static. You don't know what scene to write next.

You sigh, get up from your keyboard, go to the refrigerator. You take out some of last night's meatloaf or scoop out some ice cream. Maybe you turn on the television and watch a little TCM or some dismal talk show that fills the late morning or early afternoon slot in the vast wasteland of visual media.

Finally, you slink back to your keyboard and ... you still don't know what to write. You start to wonder whether the story itself is flawed. And if this is a novel under contract, and you have already cashed an advance check, and the deadline is, like, soon, you might also feel little trickles of sweat down your neck.

So what do you do? I have a suggestion. I call them the two writing power questions.

1. Is There Enough at Stake?

I always stress that the stakes of a story must be *death*. I talked about death earlier in this chapter. Remember, there are three kinds of death: physical, professional, and psychological/spiritual. The core issue in your novel has to be one of these or the book will not be the best it can be.

For example, in a legal thriller—the kind where the story is about a trial—that central case of the story has to be a matter of professional life and death for the lawyer. In *The Verdict*, Paul Newman is a bottom-feeding lawyer (no, that's not redundant, thank you very much). He has lost all self-respect. He drinks too much. His professional life is just about over.

And then he gets this case. A family comes to him because one of their own has been rendered a vegetable by recklessness at a large hospital. Newman thinks maybe he'll get a quick settlement, take the money and stock up on booze. But he goes to the hospital to see the poor woman. And suddenly he cares again. He realizes he is this family's only hope. Facing huge odds, he takes the case to trial.

If he loses, it'll be death to him as a lawyer.

That's how it has to feel to your lead. In a romance, the death is psychological. It has to be clear to the reader that if the two lovers don't get together, their lives will forever be damaged. They will not be complete.

Much literary, or character-driven, fiction is also of this kind. In Janet Fitch's *White Oleander*, for example, the issue is whether Astrid, tossed into the foster care system, will come out whole or irretrievably harmed.

So, make this your first power question: Are the stakes *death*? If not, back up and make it so.

2. How Can it Get Worse?

If you're stranded in a book, just ask yourself what is the next bad thing that can happen? What will make the character's situation worse?

In Scott Smith's classic, *A Simple Plan*, a normal guy falls into a scheme to score some drug money with the prospect/hope that no one will ever find out. What makes the book so compelling is that it's like a slow-motion car wreck. You keep saying to yourself, *Don't do that. Please don't do that.* And then the character does it and descends further into a pit that will eventually close around him.

Brainstorm for a while. Make a list of the bad things that can happen. Come up with ten. Then ask: What is the absolute worst thing that can happen?

Look at the list and select the best ideas. Then put them in descending order, from bad to worse to worst. That becomes a plan for writing the rest of your book.

Whether you're a pantser or an outliner, these two power questions can blast you through that wall, to the other side where completed novels grow.

HOW TO WRITE ACT II

Here's a clip from an e-mail I received some time ago (used with permission):

> This is a small point that I've wanted to ask a teacher for some time because I've noticed this situation in other structure layouts: Why is it that Act II, which constitutes at least half of the entire story (actually 55 percent if Act I is 20 percent and Act II is 25 percent), has relatively fewer structure points? And yet we're often told that the hardest part of writing a novel or screenplay *is* Act II. Is it the hardest partly because it's harder to teach in terms of structure, etc?

That's an excellent and insightful question. It does seem counter-intuitive to suggest that the *least* number of structural points occur in the longest section of the novel.

But, in point of fact, this is exactly how it must be.

First of all, what is Act II all about? It's about the lead's confrontation with death. I've discussed several times what death can entail, and it's the only thing that makes the stakes high enough for the reader to care about what's going on.

Act I prepares us for this death struggle. To get readers to care about what happens, we have to bond them with a lead character, show something of the ordinary world, have hints of trouble to come ... and then we have to find a way to *force* the lead through that Doorway of No Return. Why force? Because no one wants to confront death unless they have to (unless their name is Evel Knievel)!

That's why there are several important structural beats in Act I. We have to have a disturbance to hook the reader. We need a care package to bond the reader with the character. We need a trouble brewing beat to let the reader know there is something at stake. Finally, we need a Doorway of No Return to push the protagonist into the Act II.

Okay, now the lead is in the dark forest. To survive and get back to the castle, she'll have to defeat the forces arrayed against her. If you want a perfect illustration of this, think of *The Hunger Games*. Katniss Everdeen is taken from her ordinary world and thrust into a contest to the death, in an arena filled with obstacles and opponents.

Now, keep these two points in mind:

1. There are innumerable actions the Lead can take to gain her objective, to survive, and to ultimately defeat the opponent.

Standing at the edge of that dark forest, the Lead might go left, go right, go straight ahead, follow a sound, run from a sound, climb a tree, make a weapon, start a fire, form an alliance, fight off a monster—whatever it is, you, the author, get to choose.

2. Each subsequent action will, in some way, be a reaction to what's just happened.

If the lead breaks her leg, she won't be running in the next scene. If her love interest decides to walk out on her, she won't be singing a happy tune.

You may also find that a character refuses to do what you want. In one novel I tried to get a wife to go away to her sister's house, but she wouldn't do it. I'd planned for her to go, I tried to push her out the door, but no soap. So I had to readjust, and in this case the character was right!

In short, a more "open" Act II enables us to respond to the story *as it takes shape.*

This is true, by the way, whether you like to outline or whether you prefer to wing it.

Further, you don't need as many signposts because your scenes should have an organic logic to them. Act II is largely made up of the lead's battle plans. We know what the objective is: defeat death! In *The Hunger Games* it's physical death; in *The Catcher in the Rye,* it's psychological death; and in *The Verdict,* it's professional death.

So the lead, in Act II, takes an action to gain a foothold in this battle and suffers a setback. Now what?

She forms a *new* plan, takes a new step, reacting to and learning from the last one.

In this way you have a natural, logical, clear and compelling "plot generator." You don't need as many signposts to do that.

If you ever feel "lost" in Act II, just go back and check a few things:

- Are the stakes death?
- Is the opponent stronger than the lead?
- Is your lead using strength of will to push forward?
- Is there an easier way for your lead to solve the problem? (If so, figure out how to eliminate that possibility.)

Then brainstorm a few answers to these questions:

- How can things get worse for the lead?
- What's the worst thing that could happen to the lead?

- Can a new character come in to complicate matters even more?
- What are the enemies of the lead doing "offscreen"? That is, what actions are they taking while the reader is reading the current scene? (Asking this question is a great way to come up with plot complications.)

Soon enough, you'll be back on track with plenty of ideas for organic scenes, and rising and falling action, throughout Act II.

Then, at some point, you have to get the lead through another doorway, into Act III, where the final battle takes place. There are more signposts in Act III to guide you through this section. That's because you can't dillydally. You've got the lead going over a waterfall. You've got to get him to safety, fast. The Act III signposts have a shorter space between them, which is exactly what you need.

Make sense?

I think it was Isaac Asimov who said that he knows the beginning and the ending of his novels, but then makes up the in-between details as he goes along.

CREATE YOUR OWN TRICKS THAT CANNOT BE EXPLAINED

My uncle Bruce was a bartender for many years in Santa Barbara. Like most of the Bells, who came from (or were chased out of) Ireland in the 1700s, he has the gift of gab. He started doing close-up magic right at the bar. This proved exceedingly popular and before long he started billing himself as "Bruce the Baffling, Magician and Social Chemist."

When I was in high school, Uncle Bruce gave me a bunch of his tricks, and I started getting into magic myself. It was a pastime that continued through college. I loved the oohs and aahs coming from an audience that was close-up. There's nothing quite like a great card or coin trick, or the cups and balls classic, performed right under the noses of people sitting a few feet away.

I became good enough to perform at the famous Magic Castle in Hollywood: not for the adults at night (you really have to be great for that gig) but for the kids on Sunday afternoon.

The best part about this was that I got to hang out at the Castle and sit around with some of the most famous magicians of the day. It's a crime their names are not as well-known as performers in other wings of entertainment. But for people who know the magic world, names like Charlie Miller and Francis Carlisle are as familiar as John Steinbeck and F. Scott Fitzgerald are to writers.

And if the most famous writer of the mid-twentieth century was Ernest Hemingway, then magic's analogue was a man named Dai Vernon (1894–1992).

Vernon was around eighty when I met him. He was friendly but also uncompromising in his dedication to the art of magic. He could not stand shoddy work. He watched me perform some card tricks once for some guests (informally, sitting around, as most of the magicians do there). When an astonished patron said to me, "How did you do that?" And I said, "Very well."

That's a good line most close-up magicians use at one time or another. A short while later I did the same trick from some other people, and once again was asked the question, "How did you do that?" And once again I said, "Very well."

Dai Vernon snapped at me, "Quit using the same material all the time!" He wanted the magicians to constantly improve and to stay fresh and never get lazy.

I owned all the Dai Vernon magic books and studied them like crazy. In one of the books, he talks about a particular trick that never failed to amaze people, which he called "The Trick That Cannot Be Explained."

He named it such because the way he performed it would change, based upon the circumstances. It started with Dai writing down the name of a card on a piece of paper, folding it, and placing down on the table. Then he'd give a pack of cards to a spectator to shuffle.

A few moments later, the spectator would select a card. How he would select it would vary, according to Dai's directions. But the card would always match the one Dai had written down.

How could that possibly be, time after time? And how was it that this trick would never be performed exactly the same way twice? Well, Dai did it by utilizing all the skills he had mastered over the years, using them to manipulate the cards and also to adjust to some things the spectator did.

I could tell you what those skills are, but then I'd have to kill you. Magician's code, you see.

But it got me thinking that this is also what a skilled writer does. Using all the techniques he's mastered, he pulls off an effect based on the circumstances in his book, which will never be the same. Each novel presents its own challenges.

Now, there are some folks out there in writing land who purport to teach or inspire writers, who often treat "technique" as a dirty word. It's limiting, don't you see? It blocks your creativity, your inner genius, your wonderful little untamed self that wants to play and be brilliant! So bah on technique.

For some writers (and I proclaim them to be a tiny minority), this might be just fine advice. For the vast majority it's toxic. That is, if they want to get better and maybe start selling their writing.

The plain fact is that writing is a craft as well as an art. Where the "just go play" people get it wrong is in misunderstanding the process.

Yes, there is time for play, for disregarding "rules" or "fundamentals." It's when you're coming up with ideas, visualizing characters or cool scenes, or even writing your day's pages. This is when you can go wild. (I have found that it helps me to use a pen and paper for this part. I use a spiral notebook, the kind a college student would use, and let my pen play all over the page, making doodles, mind maps, plot ideas, and connections between characters.)

But there comes a time when you have to look at your writing and put the screws to it. And to do that, you have to know how to identify weaknesses and know the way to fix them. Like a plumber, you have to know your tools and where to use them (and believe me, the plumber metaphor is apt, because most first drafts are, well, what they are).

This is where craft study and knowledge come in.

My most valuable writing possession is a big notebook full of my notes on writing. I put it together over the first ten years of my career and have periodically added to it since. It's a compendium of the things I learned, recorded like an excited scientist discovering some new antibody or cure for baldness. Whenever I hit a little drought in the writing week I can always flip through my notes and become reenergized in about five minutes.

Do the same. Study the craft and make notes on what you learn. Create your own writer's notebook. You'll love it as the years roll on and your writing gets stronger and stronger.

And you'll especially love performing tricks that cannot be explained when you revise, because you'll be making magic for your readers.

TRICKS EXERCISES

1. When you finish your first draft, don't look at it again for at least three weeks. Longer is fine. Start working on your next project.
2. Print out a hard copy. Some writers use an e-reader or tablet, which is fine. I like paper because I can jot things down quickly.
3. Try with all your might to read it the way a reader would, as if you'd just bought this book.
4. Take minimal notes. Don't do any big fixes. Just make notes in the margin to remind you what you are thinking.
5. When you finish the first read through, ask these questions:

   a. Is there any point when a busy editor would be tempted to put this down?
   b. Are there any characters that are flat and uninteresting?
   c. Are the motives of all the major characters clear?
   d. What are the three weakest scenes? Why are they weak? Pinpoint the problems.
   e. Are the stakes high enough to sustain an entire book?

Study the ways you can address each of these problems. Record the techniques you learn. Add them to your notebook.

Part II

A REWARDING
WRITING LIFE

Chapter 5

BRAVE THE WRITING LIFE

Writing is a way of life. If you're going to commit to being a writer, and you seek success as you have defined it, you're going to have to prepare, study, act. Learn to observe with a writer's eye. Ask "What if?" about everything. Be empathetic about people so you can craft three-dimensional characters. Be true to yourself, but also expand your boundaries. Live large, for only then can you write books that connect in a big way.

DO NOT GO GENTLE ONTO THAT GOOD PAGE

> Do not go gentle into that good night ... Rage, rage against the dying of the light.
> —DYLAN THOMAS

Brett Favre, one of the best quarterbacks ever to play the game of football, was supposed to be over-the-hill at forty. But in 2010 he finished what was probably his finest season. He almost got the Minnesota Vikings to the Super Bowl.

In the NFC championship game against the New Orleans Saints, he took a beating. He was on the turf constantly, sometimes under 380 pounds of beef. In the second half, he twisted his left ankle, limped off the field, got retaped, and came back into the game. Except for a couple of turnovers by his teammates and one ill-timed interception, the Vikes would have won. It was an inspiring performance that added to his legend.

Robert B. Parker, creator of the character Spenser in his detective series, and one of the most prolific authors of our time, died that same year, at the age of seventy-seven. He was supposed to be over-the-hill, too. Some critics thought he was, but most readers did not. Parker was turning out books to the very end, and not just in his Spenser series. He had other series going, including Jesse Stone, which Tom Selleck successfully brought to television. He also wrote stand-alone novels and Westerns.

He was reportedly about forty pages into a new Spenser novel when he suffered a heart attach and died at his desk.

For a writer, that's the way to go.

For a writer, not to write is death.

At the age of ninety-seven, Herman Wouk, one of America's greatest storytellers, scored another publishing contract. For him, not writing was unthinkable. So he never stopped.

Favre, Wouk, and Parker refused to go gentle into that good night. To write well, there has to be a part of you that is determined to rage, rage against the dying of the light—and against rejection, criticism, and the slough of despond.

You've got to have some attitude.

Now, this attitude is not the same as arrogance. Arrogance shouts and gets tiresome pretty fast. Attitude is just as ornery, but it's quiet. It does its work and keeps on doing it. It wants to prove itself on the page, not via the mouth. And it refuses to give up.

A knock on Parker in the latter phase of his career was that he wrote too much, sacrificing quality. That's between him and his readers. He wrote, they bought, they enjoyed, and maybe some got frustrated. But the relationship was lasting, and the man was doing what he loved.

If you love to write, you'll find a way to do it. No one can promise how it'll turn out. No one can guarantee you a publishing contract. But you'll never get close if you don't rage a little, if you don't turn that rage into determination to keep writing, keep going, keep producing the words.

My grandfather and my mom both wanted to be writers. So they wrote. My grandfather wrote historical fiction and ended up self-publishing a few stories. I remember him being proud of it, and his books pleased the family.

My mom wrote radio scripts while she was in college during WWII. I have a whole bunch of them, and they're quite good. She worked on a small local newspaper when I was a kid. I remember, when I was twelve or so, finding a short story she wrote—a sci-fi kind of thing—that had a cool twist ending. She never got it published, but it influenced at least one young writer—me.

What I'm saying is, do not go gentle onto that good page. If you want to write, then write, and make it a write-or-die kind of thing.

You'll never know where your writing will go unless you actually write it. It's the best way to live. At the very least you'll know you're alive. You won't walk around (as Bill Murray says in *A Thousand Clowns*) with that wide-eyed look some people put on their faces so no one will know their head's asleep.

Rage a little, throw the heat, write.

There is no one to stop you but you.

So get out of your way.

WRITE BRAVE, LIVE BRAVE

Since 2009 or so, the so-called midlist at traditional publishing houses has dried up faster than a mud patch in the Serengeti. The bleached bones of writers who did not earn out are scattered in random configuration. On the parched ground near a scorched femur can be seen a message scratched in the dirt, a last call from a thirsty scribe: *Help! My numbers suck!*

I've heard from many friends and colleagues about traditionally published writers—some who have had relationships with a
house for a decade or more—seeing their advances drop to record
lows, or not being offered another contract at all.

And then what? What happens to these foundering careers?

Two writers give us answers. The first is Eileen Goudge, a *New
York Times* best-selling author. She had a soaring career in the
1990s, and even a power marriage to superagent Al Zuckerman.
That's how I became aware of her. Zuckerman wrote a good
book on writing blockbusters where he recommended reading
Goudge's *Garden of Lies*. I did and enjoyed it, and read another
of hers a bit later on.

So I was gobsmacked when I read a post written by Goudge
about her travails as a casualty of commerce in a blog post on writer and editor Jane Friedman's blog.[1] It describes what happened to
her and many other writers this way:

> I know from my husband, the aviation geek, that when a plane goes
> into what's called a death spiral, as it reaches a certain altitude and
> succumbs to the pull of gravity, it can't pull out. The same holds true
> for authors: fewer orders results in smaller print runs, a smaller mar-
> keting budget and lackluster sales, then a smaller advance for your
> next title, and the vicious cycle continues. In short, you've entered
> the "death spiral."
>
> The cold, hard truth is this: If the sales figures for your last title
> weren't impressive enough to get booksellers to order your next title
> in sufficient quantities to make an impact, you're basically screwed.
> It doesn't matter if your previous titles sold a combined six million
> copies worldwide. You're only as good as your last sell-through.
>
> What's even more dispiriting is that you're perceived as a "fail-
> ure" by publishers when your sales haven't dropped but aren't grow-
> ing. You become a flat line on a graph. The publisher loses interest
> and drops the ball, then your sales really do tank. Worse, your poor
> performance, or "track" as it's known, is like toilet paper stuck to

---

[1] https://janefriedman.com/leap-to-indie/

your shoe, following you wherever you go in trying to get a deal with another publisher.

Goudge details some of the things that happened to her, on both a personal and corporate level. One of them is fairly common: a key executive or editor, who is your champion, leaves, gets laid off, or moves to another company. You become an "orphan" at the house and your books don't get the attention they used to.

All these things were "crushing" to Goudge. She says she felt like Charlie Brown trying to kick the football. Every time she got close to something good, the ball would be snatched away.

A writer friend of hers told Goudge she should go independent. She resisted at first, but the friend simply asked, "What's the alternative?"

So Eileen Goudge jumped into the independent waters, more than a bit nervous about it. But then she discovered something wonderful:

> My creative wellspring that'd been drying up, due to all the discouragement I'd received over the past few years, was suddenly gushing. An idea for a mystery series, something I'd long dreamed of writing, came to me during a walk on the beach in my hometown of Santa Cruz, California, where I lived before I moved to New York City. Why not set my mystery series in a fictional town resembling Santa Cruz? ... I immediately got to work. I was on fire!

Goudge is professional enough and has seen enough to know that nothing is rock-solid certain in a writing career.

> Was it worth it? Only time will tell. Meanwhile there it is, beating in my breast: that feathered thing called hope. Something I thought I'd lost, regained. Something to celebrate.

Hope. I like that. Worth celebrating indeed.

Another casualty of commerce is a friend of mine, Lisa Samson. I've known Lisa for fifteen years. She is one of the most naturally gifted writers I've ever met. She's won numerous awards. She has the respect of critics and a loyal following of fans.

Right around the same time Goudge published her post, Lisa posted to her Facebook page:

> Dear Friends,
>
> All good things must come to an end, the saying goes. I, however, like to think that all good things continue to evolve. For twenty-two years I have been writing for the inspirational (read: evangelical Christian) market, and it has been an honor and a privilege. True, with the artistic strictures and the increasing necessity for a platform, it has had its share of frustrations for a novelist who simply wants to explore an art form, but sharing stories and getting to know readers as friends, hearing how these words have been used to encourage, inspire, affirm, and even challenge, has been a thrill. ...

Lisa talks about the changes in the publishing world, how publishing houses now expect authors to do most of the marketing themselves. And then there is the cold, hard economic facts of life to think of as well:

> I was recently offered a contract that was insufficient for me to support my family. A real step down from the previous one. And that is all I will say about that matter. It wasn't personal, I realize, but it was severely disappointing to have worked faithfully for two decades only to have your work go down in value to that point. I wish money didn't matter, but it has to, and that saddens me. I'm still intensely grateful for the time I spent writing for that house and the people there who are, quite simply, wonderful. But traditional publishing is a business, and I'm no good for the bottom line no matter how much I'm personally loved, and good feelings don't keep the lights on over here at my house.

Lisa admits to discouragement (as any writer at this point would), but she has a response. A deeply spiritual person, Lisa has enrolled in a massage therapy program with the aim of bringing relief to cancer, hospice, and Alzheimer's patients.

In other words, there is life away from writing. That's a crucial lesson for all writers to learn. Heck, for any professional.

Will Lisa write again? She isn't completely closing the door, and my prediction is yes. She's too good and has too much inside her not to share more stories. But she's not brooding over it. She is too busy giving of herself to others.

These two writers are strong and resilient and have chosen brave paths.

So can you. When discouragement hits, as it will, know that you are not alone and that life still offers you options.

Grab one, and go for it.

BRAVE EXERCISES

1. Write a page in your journal about what you fear about the writing life. Be honest with yourself.
2. Write a letter to yourself advising you what to do if you ever run up against a severe disappointment.
3. Finally, write a journal entry on what the most important things in life are for you personally. Make those things your "bottom line" as you shape your whole life, not just your writing life.

COMPETITION IS GOOD

For years I've bought my Apple products at the big Apple store near my home. It's located on the second floor of a large shopping mall. It majestically dominates the middle of the mall and, being near the food court and Coffee Bean, has arguably the best location in the whole place. There is even a walkway bridge that leads strolling shoppers from one side of the mall directly over to the large, open, and welcoming Kingdom of Jobs.

Some time ago my wife and I were walking through the mall when I spotted a sign alerting us that a new store had just opened. It, too, was located just off the food court. I said, "Let's go over there. I want to see it. It must be near the Apple store."

Not just near, but *directly across from the Apple store, at the other end of that same walkway bridge.*

You may have guessed that it was a new, gleaming Microsoft store.

And if so, you would be right.

I could not help noticing how, um, similar the store looks to Apple's setup: lots of tables with laptops and tablets and phones. A help desk modeled after Apple's Genius Bar. Sales staff in brightly colored T-shirts like their counterparts across the way, complete with nametags hanging around their necks shaped the same as the Apple crew's.

A year ago there was a story about Apple going after Microsoft's bread-and-butter market: i.e., business. Now it seems Microsoft is giving Apple a run for its money in the consumer market.

I note that the Microsoft space is just one-third the size of the Apple store, but it has shown up. It is here.

Game on.

Competition. It's good. Because it generally makes the free market a better place for consumers.

It also makes an individual stronger.

I grew up playing competitive sports. It taught me some lessons that I've carried with me my whole life, including the writing part. Here are three:

Somebody Always Has More Natural Talent than You Do

You cannot change what talent or physiology you're born with. When you get into competition you find that out pretty fast.

I was a great six-foot three-inch shooting guard on my high school basketball team. What I didn't have was hops. I could not dunk. If I had been six foot nine inches, maybe I would have made it to the NBA. At my height, though, I didn't have enough spring in my sticks.

So I determined to work as hard as I could with what I had. I managed not only to play at the college level, but for many years after that in recreational leagues and pickup games, just for fun.

The same goes for my writing. There are some writers out there who seem to have such a way with words that it makes me feel like a caveman carving symbols on a rock. But that just makes me want to work harder at my craft.

What talent you have is not up to you. What is up to you is what you do with it. Do you want to be someone who writes and gets paid for it? Then work at your craft. It's quite common that the harder worker overtakes the more gifted, but indolent, athlete. See Rose, Pete (look for him under "Baseball," not "Gambling").

When You Play, Play with All Your Heart

Once in the game, give it your all. Never quit.

In 1916, the Georgia Tech football team played little Cumberland College. The score was 63-0 after the first quarter. The final score was 222-0. Look it up.

At one point they found a Cumberland player wrapped in a blanket, sitting on the Georgia Tech bench. When they asked him why, he said he feared his coach would put him back in the game.

You're going to suffer through disappointments. That's part of the writing life. No matter how bad it gets, though, stay in the game. The great thing about writing is you are the only one who can stop you. So don't stop you.

Desire and determination trump disappointment. Learn what you can from setbacks. Maybe you need to work on characterization, or dialogue, or plotting. There are abundant resources to help you in every single area. Join a critique group. Go to a conference.

Just don't wrap yourself up in a blanket and never play again.

Your Ultimate Competition is Yourself

Don't waste any time comparing yourself to other writers, envying their successes (or secretly hoping they fail). That's wasted energy. Sure, entering your book in an awards competition stacks you up against other colleagues. But don't let losing (or even winning for that matter) mess with your head.

Instead, always concentrate, with all your creative might, on the page in front of you.

And forget about luck. I don't believe in believing in luck. Those who believe that bad luck is the reason for not making it are like that geezer with three days' growth of beard at the end of the bar. "I coulda been a contendah, but da breaks wuz against me!"

What good does that do?

Instead, keep fighting.

Rocky Marciano was one of the greatest boxers of all time. He won the heavyweight championship of the world and never lost a fight his entire professional career.

But his start was not so promising. Marciano, nicknamed the Brockton Blockbuster because in his youth he delivered big blocks of ice for the Brockton Ice and Coal Company, had incredibly strong arms. And those muscles were heavy; the muscles used to hold his arms up were not as developed.

The result was that after a few rounds Marciano's arms began to sag, giving his sparring partners greater access to his face.

Instead of quitting, Marciano came up with his own training routine. He went to the local YMCA pool and practiced throwing punch after punch underwater. He got a heavy bag that weighed 180 pounds (most heavy bags weigh about fifty). He threw punches at that bag for hours ... *with bare fists*. Needless to say those fists became solid granite and his arms become pile drivers.

The result? Marciano's record was 49–0, forty-five were knockouts.

He once said, "I was willing to make sacrifices. Even while traveling, when there were no facilities. I would spend hours in my hotel room working on my strength. I wanted more than anything to be a fighter. Then I wanted to be a good one, and after that a great champion."

What do you want, dear writer? What are you willing to sacrifice?

Not everyone is born with an iron will. But you can develop it. If you take baby steps every day—writing, studying, editing, writing some more—soon you'll be making longer strides.

There's an old saying in boxing that you have to keep punching, because you always have a puncher's chance.

So when you get knocked down, get right back up. Keep punching that keyboard. You always have another chance.

FROM FAILURE TO SUCCESS IN WRITING

As a young man I found Frank Bettger's *How I Raised Myself From Failure to Success in Selling* helpful. It's considered a classic of the sales-training genre. Lots of folks have given the book props for helping them get ahead in other professions, too.

The title is also apt because I definitely thought myself a failure as a writer when I was in my twenties. The stuff I wrote didn't work the way I wanted it to, and I was told that's because you have to be born a writer. You can't learn how to do it.

For ten years or so I accepted that I would never make it in this business.

So I did some other things. I moved to New York to pursue an acting career. I started doing off Broadway, Shakespeare, avant-garde. But after a while I wondered why I wasn't being offered a starring role in a movie like *Raiders of the Lost Ark* (they gave it to some guy named Ford).

During a visit back to L.A., I met this gorgeous actress at a party. Knowing I'd be returning to New York soon, I only waited two-and-a-half weeks to ask her to marry me.

Shockingly, she said yes.

After we were married, I decided it might be a good idea for us to have one steady paycheck. Since Cindy was the more talented of the two of us, she continued with her stage work while I applied to law school.

In my third year at USC Law I interviewed with a big firm with offices in Beverly Hills.

Shockingly, they hired me.

Later on I opened my own office. I then found out I had to be a businessman, too. I had to learn entrepreneurial principles. So I started to read books on business, and one of these was Bettger's.

A few years went by and the desire to write, which had burned in me since I read *Tarzan of the Apes* as a kid, came back to me. Bettger's principles helped me along that path, too.

Frank Bettger was a former big-league ballplayer who went into the insurance game. After initial failures he started wondering if he really had what it took to be a good salesman. He decided to find out what others did. He began to apply a set of practices that helped get him to the top.

The first of these practices was *enthusiasm*. To sell successfully, you have to be enthusiastic about your product, your prospects, and life itself. You need to exude joy, because the alternative is gloom, and gloom doesn't sell.

Bettger noticed that even if he didn't feel enthusiastic, he could still *act* enthusiastic, and soon enough the feeling came tagging right along.

When I discovered you really can learn the craft, I got as excited as a man in the ocean who finds a plank to hang on to and then spots a lush island in the distance. It was enough to infuse joy and hope into my writing, and those two things alone started to improve it.

Another practice Bettger mentions is a system of organization: make plans, record your results. When I got my first book contract, I hadn't thought through what I'd do for a follow-up. So I got organized. I began planning my career five years ahead, kept track of who I met with and pitched to, who I wanted to meet, and scheduled projects accordingly.

I'd already established the discipline of writing to a quota, but now I started keeping track of my output on a spreadsheet. (See "The Ten Characteristics of Highly Effective Writers," chapter seven, for advice on tracking your writing output.)

Next, Bettger summarized the most important "secret" in sales: Find out what the other fellow wants, then help him find the best way to get it.

This got me thinking about pleasing readers. In college I was heavily influenced by the Beats (Kerouac, Ginsberg, et al). Their writing was idiosyncratic and experimental. But I figured out early that idiosyncratic did not necessarily connect with a large audience.

I knew I could write solely for myself, ignore genre, and be hip (though a lot of the time it was artificial hip). But I wanted to make a living at writing, so I backed up and looked for points where my own pleasure met with readers' desire for a good story.

Still, I needed more self-confidence. Bettger wrote that the best way to increase confidence is to *keep learning about your business*. Never stop.

The same holds true for writing, both the craft side and the business side.

If you are set on traditional publishing you need to know: What are publishing contracts like? What terms are you willing to accept ... or, more important, walk away from? What are the characteristics of a good agent? What can you realistically expect in terms of editorial and marketing?

If you are going to self-publish, do you have a plan? Do you know what you need to know? Are you putting in a systematic effort to find out? Are you a risk taker?

In my business life I have dedicated at least half an hour a day to reading about business principles, and thinking and planning. I do the same in my writing life. I read every issue of *Writer's Digest*. I enjoy books and blogs on the craft. My philosophy has always been that if I pick up even just one new technique, or if I see something familiar from another point of view, my work has been worth the effort.

There's a lot more packed into Bettger's book, but I'll close with the part that helped me most, both as a businessman and as an author. It's his chapter on Benjamin Franklin's plan for self-improvement.

In Franklin's autobiography, he writes about his desire, as a young man, to acquire the habits of successful living. Franklin chose thirteen virtues, such as temperance, resolution, frugality, justice, and so on. He made a chart and concentrated on one virtue for a week, thereby ingraining the habit. Proceeding in this way, he could go through his list four times a year.

Bettger followed this plan by choosing thirteen practices that would help him as a salesman, such as sincerity, remembering names and faces, service and prospecting, and so on.

I did something similar with my writing. I formulated what I call the critical success factors of fiction (see the next heading). By concentrating on these serially, I hoped to raise my overall fiction competence. Today I would describe these as: plot, structure, character, scenes, dialogue, theme, and voice/style.

Bettger's book helped me at two crucial points in my life—when I had to run a business and when I made the decision to pursue my writing dream. In both pursuits there are challenges aplenty. Sources of inspiration are critical. I'm glad that ex-ballplayer was around to fire me up.

FAILURE TO SUCCESS EXERCISES

1. Assess your enthusiasm level when you write. When you write, can you do it without fear or some "inner voice" tossing you doubts?
2. Increase your enthusiasm by writing *as if it were impossible to fail.* Put that note of confidence in your mind when you are working on your words.
3. Have you organized your writing life? Set down a plan, in writing, for both production of words and study of craft.

THE SEVEN CRITICAL SUCCESS FACTORS OF FICTION

The following seven areas cover everything about the fiction craft. I advise all serious writers to objectively test themselves in each area, then design self-study programs to elevate each one, starting with the weakest.

A self-study should involve reading craft books on the subject, studying novels that do one or more of these particularly well, and writing practice scenes and getting feedback.

Do this systematically, and your writing will kick up several notches, guaranteed.

1. Plot

Plot is the collection of events in your novel, which form the overall narrative. It should all add up to a character's struggle with death.

Remember, death is of three types—physical, professional, psychological.

2. Structure

How your plot events line up is a matter of structure. I call structure "translation software for your imagination." What I mean is that readers need all that wonderful story material you have in you—the heart, the passion, the intensity—to be presented in a way they can follow and relate to.

All writing teachers, whether they admit it or not, espouse the three-act structure: beginning, middle, and end. The middle (or muddle) is the second act, and the longest part of the story.

Yes, you can play with structure, but know this: The further you get from traditional structure, the more you move toward the "experimental" novel. There's nothing illegal about that, but just know that experimental novels rarely break out.

3. Character

Characters are, of course, the lifeblood of fiction. All the twisty-turny plot elements in the world won't matter to readers if they are not bonded to a character they care about.

Many approaches and techniques for creating characters are out there. Some writers like to create massive backstory documents or answer a list of questions. Others prefer to create on the fly as they write.

Whatever method you use, you want your characters to be "rounded" (E.M. Forster), which means "capable of surprising us in a convincing way."

4. Scenes

Scenes are the building blocks of your novel. A plot is a collection of scenes, and scenes presented structurally form the narrative.

A scene has its own internal structure: a POV character has an objective. That objective is met by obstacles (which make for conflict). And eventually there's an outcome.

Your default on outcomes should be a setback. It makes the situation worse for the protagonist. Sometimes, for variety, the protagonist succeeds in the objective, but that victory ought to lead to more trouble down the line.

Richard Kimble in *The Fugitive* gets into a hospital to dress his wound (without being seen). He succeeds. But his decency at the end of the scene leads him to help a wounded guard, and that in turn leads to the authorities' discovery of his whereabouts, and the chase continues.

5. Dialogue

After reading many manuscripts at conferences over the years, I've come to the conclusion that dialogue is the fastest way to improve a manuscript. It's also the fastest way to sink a manuscript.

Great dialogue is compressed, differentiated among characters, and has a certain zing. I've written an entire book on the subject, *How to Write Dazzling Dialogue.*

6. Meaning

Meaning, or theme, is a "leave behind" in every novel. The only question is whether you are going to be intentional about formulating it.

Some authors begin with a theme in mind. Others find it after they've finished a draft. Still others give it no thought at all, letting the story play out as it will.

My opinion is that knowing the meaning of your story, at whatever point that knowledge comes, and weaving that meaning naturally into the plot, makes for the best reading experience.

To help get you to the meaning, imagine your main character twenty years after the events of the plot have occurred. Ask this character why she had to go through all that trouble? What life lesson did she learn that she can pass along to the rest of us?

7. Voice

Voice is one of the least understood aspects of fiction. All agents and editors say they want to find a "fresh voice," but don't know how to define it.

Here is the definition:

> *Character* background and language filtered through the *author's* heart, and rendered with craft on the page = voice

Think about it. Study it (I've written a book on voice, if you want more: *Voice: The Secret Power of Great Writing*), and take your fiction to the next level.

KEEP PUNCHING

One of my favorite movies of all time is *Somebody Up There Likes Me* starring Paul Newman. It's one of the great boxing films, a biopic of middleweight champion Rocky Graziano. We talked about him earlier, but there's a lot to be learned from boxing.

Graziano grew up in the toughest of neighborhoods, the lower East Side of New York. As the famous boxing writer Bert Sugar put it, "Graziano was raised on the Lower East Side, where both sides of the tracks were wrong."

He was a tough street kid, a delinquent whose father made him box his older brother to the point of tears. The one thing he learned growing up was to punch.

He was in and out of reform school, and in and out of the Army. When he finally needed a way to make some money, he turned to boxing and became a legendary knockout artist. Eventually, he won the World Middleweight Championship, but it was not easy.

His opponent was another great champion, Tony Zale. Zale had defeated Rocky in their previous fight, and in this one he again savaged Graziano. The referee was about to stop the fight, but Rocky's cut man managed to stop the bleeding.

It looked like it was curtains for Rocky Graziano once again.

But the one thing he could do was punch. And there was no quit in him.

In the sixth round, he put Tony Zale down for good.

He had that puncher's chance.

My friends, this is true for anything you want to do. You have to keep punching. The only other option is to give up.

Do you have quit in you?

Then dump it. Because if you keep writing, keep learning, keep growing, you have a chance to make something of this writing life.

WRITE UNTIL YOU DIE

As discussed in the opening section of this chapter, I've always loved those writers like Herman Wouk who never stopped writing, who kept on pounding away until the very end (Herman had a book come out at the age of 97). I want to be like when the deep winter of life rolls around. Still writing. Still dreaming. Still publishing. Thus I was intrigued by a story with the provocative title "Is Creativity Destined to Fade with Age?" by Tara Bahrampour of The Washington Post.[2] It begins:

> Doris Lessing, the freewheeling Nobel Prize–winning writer on racism, colonialism, feminism and communism who died recently at age 94, was prolific for most of her life. But five years ago, she said the writing had dried up.
>
> "Don't imagine you'll have it forever," she said, according to one obituary. "Use it while you've got it because it'll go; it's sliding away like water down a plug hole."

Lessing had a stroke in the 1990s, which may have contributed to her outlook. Does that mean older writers are destined to have a dry well? One researcher cited in the article (Mark Walton, author of *Boundless Potential: Transform Your Brain, Unleash Your Talents, Reinvent Your Work in Midlife and Beyond*) says no:

> What's really interesting from the neuroscience point of view is that we are hard-wired for creativity for as long as we stay at it, as long as nothing bad happens to our brain.

Another researcher, Michael Merzenich, professor emeritus of neuroscience at the University of California at San Francisco and author of *Soft-Wired*, a book about optimizing brain health, added a caveat:

> [R]epeating the same sort of creative pursuit over the decades without advancing your art can be like doing no exercise other than sit-ups your whole life.

[2] http://www.vnews.com/lifetimes/9566509-95/is-creativity-destined-to-fade-with-age

> [One-trick artists] become automatized, they become very habit-borne. They're not continually challenging themselves to look at life from a new angle.

This is one reason I love self-publishing options. Writers can play. We can go where we want to go without being tied to one brand or type of book. We can write short stories, novelettes, novellas, novels, and series. When I'm not working on suspense, I like to challenge myself with a different voice for my boxing stories, my kick-butt nun novelettes, or my zombie legal thrillers. I'm currently planning a collection of short stories that will be of the weird Fredric Brown variety. Why? Because I can, and because it keeps my writing chops sharp.

This appears to be the key to this whole longevity business:

> Older artists can also be galvanized by their own sense of mortality. Valerie Trueblood, 69, a Seattle writer who did not publish her novel, *Seven Loves*, and two short story collections until her 60s, said age can bring greater urgency to the creative process.
>
> "I think for many older people there's a time of great energy," Trueblood said. "You see the end of it, you just see the brevity of life more acutely when you're older, and I think it makes you work harder and be interested in making something exact and completing it."

People with regular jobs usually can't wait to retire. A writer should never retire. Fight to be creative as long as you live. Do it this way:

Always Have at Least Three Projects Going

I think all writers should, at a minimum, have three projects on the burner: their work in progress; a secondary project that will become the WIP when the first is completed; and one or more projects "in development" (notes, concepts, ideas, character profiles, etc.). This way your mind is not stuck in one place.

Take Care of Your Body

The writer's mind is housed in the body, so do what you have to do to keep the house in shape. Start small if you have to. Eat an apple every day. Drink more water. Walk with a small notebook and pen, ready to jot notes and ideas.

Stay Positive and Productive

Write something every day. Even if it's just an entry in your journal. Know that what you write to completion will see publication, guaranteed. It may be via a contract, like Herman Wouk. Or it may be digitally self-published. Heck, it could be a limited printing of a memoir, just for your family. Or a blog. Writers write with more joy when they know they will be read, and joy is one key to memorable prose.

Rage, rage against the dying of the light. Do so on your keyboard. Refuse to believe you have diminished powers or have in any way lost the spark that compelled you to write in the first place. If someone tells you that you just don't have it anymore, throw your teeth at them. Who gets to decide that? You do. And your answer is, *I've still got it, baby, and I'm going to show you with this next story of mine ...*

You're a writer! So write and never decompose.

DON'T SABOTAGE YOUR WRITING

This writing life has enough gremlins—rejection, bad reviews, economic uncertainty, short actors playing your six-foot-five-inch hero in a movie version—that a writer should be careful not to add his own. Here are ten ways you may be sabotaging your own writing.

Thinking About Your Career More than Your Writing

Guess what? No matter where you are in your writing career you can always find a reason to be unhappy about it. You're unagented and you want to get an agent. You're unpublished and you want to be published. You're published and you want to be *read*. You're read but not read in the numbers you hoped. You've gone independent and your books aren't selling enough to buy you a monthly mocha.

You can always find something to be unhappy about. What you ought to do is write more. When you're into your story and you're pounding the keys and you're imagining the scene and you're feeling the characters, you're not camping out in the untamed country of unfulfilled expectations.

The Comparison Trap

What good is it going to do you to look at somebody else's success and hit the table and cry out for justice? Writing is not *just*. It just *is*. You do your work the best you can and you let the results happen, because you can't manipulate them. You can't touch them, you can't change them, you can't fix them. You can only give it your best shot each time out.

> "There is only one way to happiness and that is to cease worrying about things which are beyond the power of our will."
> —EPICTETUS

Ranking Obsession

Another thing you can't control is your ranking on Amazon or the various and sundry best-seller lists. Sure, there are things writers do to try and "game the system." The paid reviews scandal of a few years ago was one of the more egregious examples of this. But in the end, game playing is not worth the knot in the stomach.

Don't worry about rankings and lists. Worry about your word count, plot, and characters. If you do the latter well, the former will take care of itself.

Envy

Another useless emotion which nonetheless seems to be a part of most writers' lives. Anne Lamott and Elizabeth Berg both lost friendships over it. Envy has even driven authors to set up sock puppet identities not merely to hand themselves good reviews, but to leave negative reviews for their rivals' books.

The Bible says, "A heart at peace gives life to the body, but envy rots the bones." (Prov. 14:30). Try to have a heart at peace by getting back to your story while, at the same time, developing the next one. That's right. Become a mini studio. Have projects "in development" even while you work at the one you've given the "green light."

Trying to be the Next James Patterson ...

Or J.K. Rowling, or Michael Connelly. Wait a second. We already have those. And they are the best at being who they are.

Become the leading brand of you, not the generic brand of someone else sitting on the shelf at the dollar store.

I'm not saying don't write in the same genre or don't try to do some of the good things other writers do. We can certainly learn from those we admire.

But when we write, we have a picture in our heads, a sort of writer self-image. And if we imagine our books being treated like Connelly's books, or we see ourselves in *Los Angeles* magazine interviewed like Connelly, we'll just end up writing like a second-rate Connelly.

Do that and you stifle the thing that has the chance to set you apart—your own voice. That's what needs to get out. That's the thing that will keep your from the "same old, same old" reaction you'll get if you're trying to be the next Whoever.

"I'm Not Good Enough to Make It."

That's not the issue. The issue is, do you *want* to write? Do you *really*? Do you want it so much that if you don't write you're going to feel diminished in some way for the rest of your life?

You should feel like you don't really have a choice in the matter. Writing is what you must do, even if you hold a full-time job, even if you chase a passel of kids around the house. You find your time and you keep writing. Keep looking to improve. You *can* improve. I've got hundreds of letters from people who validate this point.

Katniss Everdeen did not think she was good enough to win the Hunger Games. But she had no choice. The writing game is an arena and once you're in, don't waste precious time worrying about how good you are. Gather your weapons and supplies, and fight.

Fear

Fear of failing. Fear of looking foolish. Fear of what your writing might say about you. We are actually wired for fear. It's a survival mechanism.

It has a good side *so long as it is not allowed to go on.* In fact, when you fear something in your writing, it may be a sign that this is the place you need to go. This is where the fresh material may be. What you are hesitant to write is in you for some reason. What is it? Write it out first, assess it later.

Once again, action (writing) is the answer. Emerson said, "Do the thing you fear, and the death of fear is certain."

Hanging on to Discouragement

When my son was first pitching Little League baseball, he'd get upset when someone got a key hit or homer off him. This would affect the rest of his performance. So I gave him a rule. I told him he could say "Dang it!" once, and hit his glove with his fist. This became the "one Dang It rule." It helped settle him down, and he went on to a great season and a victory in the championship game.

When discouragement comes to you, and it will, go ahead and feel it. Say "Dang it!" (Or, if you're alone, exercise your freedom of speech as you see fit.) But time yourself. Give yourself permission to feel bad for thirty minutes. After that, go to the keyboard and start writing again.

Loving the Feeling of Being a Writer More Than Writing

The most important thing a writer does, said the late Robert B. Parker, is produce. Don't fall into the trap of writing a few words in a journal, lingering over the wonderful vibrations of being alive with the tulips of creativity budding within your brain, and leaving it at that.

You've got to get some sweat equity going in this game. I don't mean you have to crank it out like some pulp writer behind in his rent (though I like this model myself). But you do have to have some sort of quota, even if it is a small one. Writing only when you "feel like it" is not the mark of a professional.

Letting Negative People Get to You

Illegitimi non carborundum. "Don't let the bastards get you down."

Next time that know-it-all says you just haven't got the stuff to be a writer, smile and repeat this Latin phrase. And as he looks at you, puzzled, turn your back, get to your computer, and proceed to prove him wrong.

And plan to make the next twelve months the most productive of your writing life.

EVEN WRITERS GET THE BLUES

All writers, like most artists, are prone to highs and lows of the mind. One of the best things I ever wrote is a short story, "I See Things Deeply," about a crazy uncle who was a poet, and suffered for it. But—*But!*—in return he saw things most men never see. He experienced life in a way that was richer and more colorful than the poor conformists who trudge through existence in the tight shoes of the ordinary.

This is also the theme of Peter Shaffer's play *Equus*. I was lucky enough to see a production starring Anthony Hopkins and Tom Hulce. It's about a psychiatrist trying to help a disturbed stable boy with a horse fixation. In probing the boy's demons, the doctor is forced to look at his own rather dull life. What has he sacrificed by being so (to put it bluntly) normal?

At one point, he says, "But that boy has known a passion more ferocious than any I have felt in my life. And let me tell you something, I envy it. That's what his stare has been saying to me all this time: At least I galloped, when did you?"

Still, there is a cost to such vision. A multipublished friend of mine recently wrote this in an e-mail (used with permission):

> I do get blue and I do have doubts about being a fake or writing a good book. I get moody. I want to be alone at times. Other times I want to be a social butterfly. It's a constant battle and sometimes I win. Other times, I just let the blues take over and wait for the fog to lift. Then I go back to my own little world where they at least understand me. I'm no Zelda, but ... I sure understand her fears.

Furthermore, we writers have many opportunities to sabotage ourselves. There are a myriad of things we can get anxious about: *Am I any good at all? Why did that reader give me one star? How can I get anybody to notice my book? Why can't I get an agent? Why is so-and-so doing so much better than I am? What's my Amazon rank today? That's my Amazon rank?*

So it seems that the "writing blues" are a necessary adjunct to the artistic enterprise. But there are some things we can do to keep them from running roughshod over us.

Learn to Be Grateful for What You've Got

So you've self-published a novel and have only five downloads this year. First of all, realize you have been given a gift—the gift of getting your book out there for potential readers, of which you now have five (and, yes, we *will* count your brother-in-law). Start by being grateful that you can type, that you can tell stories, that your imagination is on the move, and that you can learn to be a better writer. Which leads to my next piece of advice:

Set Up and Follow a Rigorous Self-Study Program

The nice thing about writing is that there are abundant resources available for you to get stronger in the craft. When you work at something, you're being proactive. Activity is one sure way to drive the blues away. Do this: Take an objective look at your writing (you may need an outside source, like a freelance editor, for this). Determine the three weakest areas in your writing (Plotting? Style? Characterization? Dialogue?) and find resources on those subject that you can study. Practice the techniques you learn.

I guarantee it will make you feel better. I love the craft and still study it diligently, but also remember this:

Write Wild on Your First Drafts

You know all about the "inner editor" who needs to be silenced when you write. Don't think too much when you're actually composing. That was Ray Bradbury's great advice. He would start in the morning, and the writing would "explode." Then he spent the latter part of the day picking up the pieces.

Give each scene you write the most creative and wild investment you can muster.

Write hot. Then edit cool.

Know You Are Not Alone

If you haven't already, sometime soon you'll get a case of the "review blues." You are in good company. No writer is immune. "If you were to ask me what *Uncle Vanya* is about," wrote a critic of Chekov's classic, "I would say about as much as I can take."

Andrew Davidson got a rave review from *Publishers Weekly* for his debut novel, *The Gargoyle:*

> Starred Review. At the start of Davidson's powerful debut, the unnamed narrator, a coke-addled pornographer, drives his car off a mountain road in a part of the country that's never specified ... Once launched into this intense tale of unconventional romance, few readers will want to put it down.

Yet *Entertainment Weekly* said:

> Doubleday ponied up a reported $1.25 million for Andrew Davidson's debut novel, *The Gargoyle*—and if they were paying for just the unintentionally hilarious sentences, that would work out to about $10,000 per howler. This much-hyped book is eye-bulgingly atrocious ...

Knowing that no matter how good a book is, it will have critics, is sure to help you at some point in your writing journey.

Then there are sales blues. All writers (even the biggies) face the sales blues, as well as the envy blues, and the who-am-I-fooling blues and all variations thereon. Which is why many a writer of the past turned to the demon rum for solace. Bad bargain. Instead:

Try Exercise

It works. Get those endorphins pumping.

Another thing I do between writing stints: lie on the floor with my feet up on a chair. Then deep breathe and relax for about ten minutes. The blood flows to the gray cells and gives them a bath. The boys in the basement get to work. And I feel energized when I get up.

You're a storyteller and the world needs stories—even if you have to slog through the swamp of melancholy to tell them. In fact, it may be that this very dolefulness is the mark of the true artist.

So stay true. Stay focused. And keep writing.

AVOIDING WRITING PARALYSIS DUE TO OVERANALYSIS

Not too long ago, I received a lengthy e-mail from a writer who has attended my workshops in the past. He gave me permission to paraphrase the gist of his lament.

This writer has worked on his craft for years and felt he was making progress. He produced three novels, and at a conference had good feedback from an editor with a big publishing house. This editor told him it was not a matter of if, but when, he would get a contract from them. He was invited to submit at any time.

That was three years ago. He has still not submitted anything.

What happened? He describes it as "paralysis by overanalysis."

> I cannot seem to get past the prison of being perfect in the first draft. Like writer's block, it's a horrible place to reside. Sometimes it's paralyzing to start. At other times its critical negative talk in my mind remembering those sessions I attended.

The sessions he mentions came from joining a local critique group. Unfortunately this was one of those groups that was run by a large ego. The group sessions seemed mostly to be about "building themselves up by tearing down others." Though this writer had great feedback from beta readers, his confidence was completely shaken as his pages were systematically massacred in the meetings. He finally left the group, but ...

> ... I'm left with a nagging residual feeling that whatever I am writing is not good enough. I continue to write and rewrite my first chapters, never satisfied they're "good enough" to move on. Even though I've

not lost the love of the story and series, I have lost confidence in my writing.

Finally, he asks:

> Are we wrestling ourselves to be so perfect in a first draft we do not allow for a full first draft to later tackle or add (or subtract) to or from in revision? And why are we so pressured to get it perfect in the first draft? What can we learn or do to get out of that futile mental process?

I wrote him back with some advice. It is based on Heinlein's Two Rules for Writing and Bell's Corollary.

HEINLEIN'S TWO RULES FOR WRITING:

1. You must write.
2. You must finish what you write.

BELL'S COROLLARY

3. You must fix what you've written, then write some more.

You Must Write

Like the old joke goes: If you have insomnia, sleep it off. And if you suffer from writer's block, write yourself out of it.

With the paralysis-by-overanalysis type of block, your head is tangling itself up in your fingers, like kelp on a boat propeller. The motor is chugging but you're not moving. You've got to cut away all that crud.

How?

First, write to a quota. I know some writers don't like quotas, but all the professional writers who made a living in the pulp era knew their value. Yes, it's pressure, but that's what you need to get you past this type of block.

Second, mentally give yourself permission to write dreck. Hemingway said that all first drafts were [dreck]. So tell yourself that before you start to write. "I can write dreck! Because I can fix it later!"

Third, do some morning writing practice. Write for five minutes without stopping, on any random thing. Open a dictionary at random and find a noun and write about that. Write memoir glimpses starting with "I remember ..."

If you're an extreme paralysis case, try a dose of Dr. Wicked's "Write or Die." This nifty little online app (you can also purchase an inexpensive desktop version) makes you write fast or begins spewing a terrible noise at you. Set your own goal (e.g., 250 words in seven minutes) and then *go*.

You are teaching yourself to be free to write when you write.

You Must Finish What You Write

I always counsel writers to write their first drafts as fast as they comfortably can. This means:

1. You only lightly edit your previous day's work, then move on and write to your quota.
2. You step back at twenty thousand words and make sure your fundamental structure is sound. Are the stakes high enough? Are you through the first Doorway of No Return?
3. Then you push on and finish.

You Must Fix What You've Written ...

The time to dig into a manuscript is after it's done. Put your first draft away for at least three weeks. Then sit down with a hard copy and read the thing as if you were a reader with a new book.

Take minimal notes. Read through it with one question in mind: "At what point would a busy reader, agent, or editor be tempted to put this aside?"

Work on that big picture first.

Read it through again looking at each scene. Here is where craft study comes in. It's like golf. When you play golf, just play. Don't think of the twenty-two things to remember at the point of impact on a full swing. After the round is when you look back and decide what to work on in practice. And when you have a good teacher to help, you learn the fundamentals and you get better.

It's the same with writing. There are good teachers who write good books, articles, and blogs, and lead workshops. Learn from them. Use what you learn to fix your manuscript *after your first draft is done.* When you write your next book, those lessons will be in your "muscle memory." You'll be a better writer from the jump.

And here I should issue a general warning about critique groups. As with everything in life, there's the good, the bad, and the ugly. If you find a good, supportive critique group, fantastic. But know there are toxic critique groups, too. Those are usually dominated by one strong voice, with iron-fisted rules about what can never be done, like: *Never open with dialogue! No backstory in the first fifty pages! Don't mention anything about the weather in the first two pages!*

Occasionally the overriding tone is set for ripping apart manuscripts and soon enough, if you've fallen victim to such a group, you'll freeze up over every sentence you write. That's what happened to this particular writer, my correspondent.

Paying for a good, experienced editor at some point is worth it. How do you find one? Research and referrals. An abundance of editors out there who used to work for New York houses have gone freelance thanks to past years of staffing cutbacks. The cost isn't minimal. Expect between one and two grand. If that's beyond your budget, then hunt down and nurture a good, solid group of beta readers.

Then Write Some More

The name of this game is production. My correspondent mentioned a writer he knows who spent eight years workshopping and conferencing the same book, until realizing it would have been much better to write eight books instead.

Make a book per year your minimum goal. If you want to be a professional writer you have to be able to do at least that. Is it easy? No. If it was, your cat would be writing novels. But as Richard Rhodes put it, "A page a day is a book a year." One book page is 250 words.

Just write.

The good news is I got an e-mail from this author after I answered him and he had this to say:

> I spent the bulk of Tuesday at the keyboard and wrote/fixed about 4,500 words in one of four sessions. I feel liberated and just wanted to thank you. So thank you. Your Rx for my dilemma has been like a reset button. One long overdue.

May it be the same for you, should you ever get a case of paralysis due to overanalysis.

Chapter 6

STUDY THE CRAFT

When in doubt, just write. Write your way out of a corner, out of your fears, out of your setbacks. It's a good default setting. But right up alongside it put another track: the study of the craft. Make constant and never-ending improvement a goal just as important as your daily pages. Just write and keep learning—these are the two steel rails that will carry you to a productive career.

MAKING A NOVEL A PAGE-TURNER

Sometime back, I started reading an old pulp novel with no great expectation. But I got pulled into the fictive dream and did not want to put the book down. I set everything else aside so I could finish the book.

I can't remember the last time that happened. Usually when I read fiction, part of my mind is analyzing it: *Why is the author doing that? Does this metaphor work? Why am I thinking of putting the book down? Ooh, that was a neat technique, I need to remember it ...*

This time, though, I was fully into the story. It was only when I finished the book I asked myself, *What just happened? Why was I so caught up? What did this author do right?*

The novel is *Big Red's Daughter*. It's a 1953 Gold Medal paperback original. I found it when I was poking around the Internet for 1940s and 1950s noir. I love that period because the plotting is often superb, the writing workmanlike to excellent, and the effect every bit as suspenseful as anything written today—without the need for gratuitous language or description of body parts. The sexual tension was suggested, even on the book covers. Oh, those covers! Love 'em.

And then I looked at the author's name. I didn't know him. So I did a little research and found out there's very little information available on John McPartland. I love discovering little-known authors, and McPartland certainly qualifies. So how pleased was I when I got the book and had this can't-put-it-down experience?

I'm not claiming that this is a novel that should have won the Pulitzer. But it is a prime example of what pulp and paperback writers of that era had to do to eat: write entertaining, fast-moving, popular fiction.

They knew the craft of storytelling. Since I teach it and analyze it myself, I was anxious to try to discover what McPartland brought to *Big Red's Daughter*. Here's what I found:

A Decent Guy Just Trying to Find His Place in the World

Jim Work is a Korea veteran, back home now and about to go to college on the G. I. Bill. The returning vet trying to find his place is a vintage postwar noir theme, one the reading audience couldn't get enough of. He wants a job. Wants to get along. Wants to find a girl and get married.

For a page-turner, you have to have a lead character that readers are not just going to care about, but also root for. Even if you're writing about a negative lead (e.g., Scrooge), the audience has to see something possibly redeeming in the character.

Jim Work is not perfect. Readers don't respond to perfect. But we are on his side, because *he yearns to do the right things*.

The Trouble Starts on Page One

Here's the first page:

> He was driving an MG—a low, English-built sports car—and he was a tire-squeaker, the way a wrong kind of guy is apt to be in a sports car. I heard the squeal of his tires as he gunned it, and then I saw him cutting in front of me like a red bug. My car piled into his and the bug turned over, spilling him and the girl with him out onto the street.
>
> By the time our iron touched I'd swung my car to the right, so it wasn't much of a crash. I climbed out in a hurry, angry and ready to go.

The MG pilot was up and ready to go, too. The girl was beside him, brushing the skirt over her long legs. Nobody drew even a scratch out of the bump.

This was a tall, lean lad with a pale face and hot, dark eyes. I saw that much before his left fist smashed into my face. Not a Sunday punch—a real fighter's hard, straight left.

I was looking up at the cloud-rimmed blue sky. My face was numb; this boy had a solid, exploding punch. I tried to roll over fast—stomping on the down man's face is popular these days. I was right but I was slow. I saw the heel coming down and I brought my hands up. But the heel swung back from me and I pushed up into a low crouch.

The girl had him from behind, pulling his jacket down over his wide shoulders, her right knee high in the small of his back. This was a girl who must have seen action. She knew just the trick to keep her boy friend from grinding my nose into my teeth with his heel.

The MG driver is Buddy Brown. The girl is Wild Kearney (her real name—love it!). And immediately Jim is drawn to her—a love interest. She is a "bronze-blonde" but "looked like the kind of girl that would be with winners, not losers, top winners in the top tournaments and never the second-flight or the almost-good-enough. Not the kind of girl that I'd ever known."

So here we have both violence and potential romance from the start. And the lead is vulnerable in both toughness and love.

The rule here is simple: Don't warm up your engines. Get the reader turning the page not because he's patient with you, but because he needs to find out what is going to happen next.

Unpredictability

Buddy Brown calms down and invites Jim out to a house where some other people are having a party. Suddenly this Brown fellow seems like he might be okay. Jim goes along because he has a desire to work Brown over for the sucker punch and possibly to start the process of getting the girl away from him.

Brown's behavior throughout the book is unpredictable, and not only that, we sense an undercurrent of danger. He's like a snake that seems friendly but could bite at any moment. You're just not sure what he's going to do next, because he is ...

A Nasty But Charming Bad Guy

Buddy Brown is ruthless and sadistic, yet able to charm the ladies and the gents. At the house party Jim calls him a "punk," and Brown says he is going to kill Jim for that remark. Jim tries to fight him again, and Brown beats him up but good. We get the sense Buddy could kill Jim without a second thought, but then he relents and is charming again.

In Hitchcock thrillers the most charming character is often the bad guy (e.g., Joseph Cotten in *Shadow of a Doubt* and Robert Walker in *Strangers on a Train*). Such a character is much more interesting than a one-note evil villain. Which leads to ...

Sympathy for the Bad Guy

Dean Koontz is big on this. The way it works is that you put in just enough backstory to understand why a guy would turn out this bad way. A reader's crosscurrent of emotion is experienced rather than analyzed, and that's a good thing. Great fiction is, above all, an emotional ride.

In one scene, Jim finds Buddy drunk and stumbling around because he knows Big Red Kearney (Wild's tough-guy father) wants to hunt him down and kill or ruin him. Jim, in a display of 1950s loyalty to his species (sober men take care of drunken men), takes Buddy into a place for coffee. Buddy then reveals a little of his backstory. When he was fifteen, growing up in New York, he and two friends got on the bad side of a local gang leader:

> [Buddy] looked across the booth at me, his bruised, pale face a little twisted.
>
> "Mick and me, we run off from home. The boys came to my house and worked over my old man to tell where I was. He didn't know, so they gave him the big schlammin. He's never going to get over it. They caught Mick downtown somewhere and they took him out on

Long Island, tied him up with wire, and burned him. You know, with gasoline. He was a very sharp kid, good dancer, lot of laughs when he was high on sticks. He got burned up."

The slender, drunken boy was talking in his soft whisper, his eyes far away from mine, talking with a clear earnestness as if he were living it all again.

"I've never forgotten that year. I hid down near the produce market, sleeping in the daytime, going out at night to scrounge rotten fruit and stuff. The big rats would be out at night and I'd carry a stick and a sack of rocks. For two months I hid like that. Then it cleared up. The wheel got sent up for armed robbery and the other guys forgot about it. But I remember that year."

Suddenly Buddy is humanized. Not that he's any less dangerous. Our emotional involvement in the story thus deepens.

A Spiral of Trouble

In the first two chapters this guy Jim has a car accident, gets punched in the face, is drawn to another man's girl, goes to a party where he gets in another fight with Buddy, and ends up badly beaten and bloody.

And this is the good part of his next couple of days. Meeting Buddy in a bar, the conversation doesn't go so well. Buddy says, 'You're a punk."

"You keep calling me that, boy, but you don't stand up to it very good. I'll tell you something. I'm going to make you crawl across the dirt to me begging me not to hurt you any more. Crawling and begging. Can you see it? Is it a picture to you?"

"Let's go back to the alley."

He laughed. His left hand snaked across the table and he had the second finger of my right hand in his fist, bending it back, holding my palm hard against the table. His right hand thrust his cigarette toward my eyes and I ducked my head back. Still torturing my finger with his left hand hard on my right, he moved up like a cat and his fingers laced into my short hair. He pulled my head way back and I tried to reach him with my left hand. He let go and clipped me across the throat with the side of his right hand. A hard clip on the Adam's apple.

It was all pain. I couldn't breathe. I couldn't move. I was in the chair, my head hanging forward, loose, holding myself up on my elbows. I could see the puddles of beer on the tabletop, I could feel the frantic pounding of my heart.

Maybe nobody noticed. It happened inside of ten seconds. I was sick and weak, knowing only the ultimate desperation of trying to get air through my paralyzed throat to my lungs.

He didn't say anything until he thought I could hear him again. Then he said, "You're probably a good man, a real good man, fighting boys like yourself. Don't feel bad. You don't have it, that's all. In about five minutes you'll be able to talk again. Then we'll talk about Broadway Red, where you met him, how well you know him. Then we'll talk about Wild, about how she's crazy about me. Then we'll go to some quiet place and I'll work you over until you crawl to me. Then we'll say good-by and that will be the end of our friendship. You can write to me if you want to."

I was there in the chair, my head hanging forward, the pain easing a little.

Somebody had walked up to the table. "Is your friend all right?" It sounded like Henry's voice.

"He choked on something. Swallowed his beer wrong."

Notice the writing in this scene. It's violent but not overwritten. McPartland allows the action to do its work and the character to tell us how it feels.

A Love Triangle

Between Wild, Buddy, and Jim. And while we're on the subject, want to see how the best writers wrote about sex back then? Here is the only sex scene in the book, in its entirety:

I swung the car to the right on the rutted road over the dune, toward the surge of the waters of the bay.

It was a finding without a knowing. There had been a typhoon in Tokyo once when the wood-and-paper buildings ripped before the fury. This was a typhoon between two people—a man and a woman who thought she belonged to another man.

Then it was a knowing as enemies who were once friends might know each other.

After that it was a silence between two people who should not have been silent. We both knew now, we understood each other. We should not have been silent in that way. At last I held her in my arms again, and there was no storm, but there were no words.

The author didn't need to describe body parts.

A Crisp Style

McPartland's style never gets in the way of the narrative. He doesn't strain for effect, and the resulting emotions are rendered naturally, sharply. After the sex scene described above, Jim takes Wild home.

She opened the door and was outside the car.

I was out and we stood there together. I brought her to me, but she was not with me. A tall girl in my arms, a lovely girl, a girl behind a frozen wall, a girl who did not speak.

Wild stood there after I put my arms down, and then there was a kiss, and we were close and warm there in the darkness, kissing as lovers do when the good-bye could be forever. Perhaps Wild thought it would be.

It was over, still without words, and she went down the steps and pushed open the door. There was a rectangle of soft light just before the door closed behind her.

I was halfway in the car when I heard the scream.

Do you want to read on? I think you do.

A Relentless Pace with a Tightening Noose

The action of the story is compressed into a couple of days, so it really moves. Any time you can put time pressure on your characters (the "ticking clock") it's a good thing. And the stakes, as previously mentioned, have to be death. In *Big Red's Daughter*, it's physical. A noose (Jim is accused of murder) is tightening around the lead's neck.

In the midst of the action there are emotional beats, too. But these never bog down the story, they only deepen it. At one point Jim is put in a jail cell. Here is the longest emotional beat in the book:

> The night loneliness engulfed me. I thought of Buddy Brown.
>
> They'd find him somewhere tonight. Walking on a dark street between the hills. In his bed. Sitting alone in his room with a bottle. Sitting alone and laughing, with the brown cigarette cupped in his hand, the weed-sweet smell thick in the room. Maybe now an officer, hand on his holstered gun, was walking toward Buddy Brown in the lonely Greyhound waiting room at Salinas while the heavy-eyed soldiers and huddled Mexicans watched. Maybe a state highway patrol car was flagging down the MG on 101. Night thoughts. Night thoughts on a bunk, scratching flea bites.
>
> They wouldn't find him. It was a night truth, one of those things that you know as you lie awake toward dawn. Maybe they'd look for him, but they wouldn't find him.
>
> I moved restlessly on the sagging bunk.

Honor

In *Revision & Self-Editing for Publication*, I wrote a section called "The Secret Ingredient: Honor." I think we are hardwired to look for honor in others and to want to act honorably ourselves when the chips are down. When Big Red Kearney shows up in the story, there is a bond of honor that he strikes with Jim, recognizing that Jim is not a punk like Buddy Brown. When this bond comes to light, it makes you root for Jim all the more.

A Resonant Ending

I won't describe what it is, lest you want to read the book. The last chapter is short, doing its job and no more. There is no anticlimax. And for my money, it ends just right, with what I call resonance. It's that feeling of satisfaction that the last note is perfect and extends in the air after you close the book.

I work on my endings more than any part of my stories. I want to leave the reader feeling like the whole trip has been worth it, right up to and including the very last line. I will sometimes rewrite my last pages ten, twenty, even thirty times.

I'm not saying these eleven items are the only way to write a page-turner, but if you can get all of them in a book, a page-turning result would be practically guaranteed.

YOU HAVE TO LEARN TO WRITE

I was sitting contentedly at one of my branch offices (with the round green sign and coffee service) when I overheard a curly-headed young man say, "The only way to learn how to write is to write!"

His female companion nodded with the reverential gaze of the weary pilgrim imbibing the grand secret of the universe from a wizened guru on a Himalayan summit. I dared not break the soporific spell. Even so, I was tempted to slide over and say, "And the only way to learn how to do brain surgery is to do brain surgery."

Friends, it is too simplistic to say, "Writing makes you a better writer." That's only partially right. It might make you a better typist. But most writers want to produce prose that other people will actually buy. For that you need more than a clacking keyboard, as essential as that may be to the career-minded writer.

Bobby Knight, the legendary basketball coach and tormenter of referees, had a wise saying: "Practice doesn't make perfect. Perfect practice makes perfect."

That's so true. If what you ingrain in your muscle memory are bad habits, you are not moving toward competence in your sport. In point of fact, you're hurting your chances of becoming the best you can be. You have to learn, and then keep writing. But you always have to be learning and studying along the way.

When I was learning basketball, I made sure my shot was fundamentally sound: elbow in, hands properly placed, perfect spin on the ball. I became one of the great shooters of my generation, or at least in the history of Taft High School.

By way of contrast, I'd play against kids who had goofy, elbow-out, sidespin shots that had never been analyzed or tweaked. These players were never a long-term threat.

So, let's get a few things straight about getting better at this craft:

You Learn to Write by Learning How to Write

As a kid I'd check out basketball books from the library and study them. Then I'd practice what I studied on my driveway. I'd watch players like Jerry West and Rick Barry, and observe their technique. Later on, I received coaching, and I once went to John Wooden's basketball camp. I played in endless pickup games, and afterward I'd think about how I played and what I could do to improve.

Writers learn their craft by reading novels and picking up techniques. They also learn by reading books on writing. Then they practice what they have learned. They get coaching from editors and go to writers conferences. They write every day and, after they write, they think about how they wrote and what they can do to improve.

Creativity and Craft Go Together

Every now and then some self-designated teacher somewhere will act the contrarian, and say a writer should forget about "rules" and the study of craft. Rules only choke off your creativity. Burn all those Writer's Digest books!

It's a silly straw man argument.

First, they use the word *rules* as if writing craft teachers (such as your humble correspondent) lay them out as law. But no one ever does that. We talk about the *techniques that work because they have been proven to do so over and over again in books that sell.* And even if a technique is so rock solid someone calls it a rule, we always allow that rules can be broken if—and only if—you know why you're breaking them and why doing so works better for your story.

What creativity mavens should endorse is this: Creativity and the "wild mind" (Natalie Goldberg's phrase) are the *beginning*, but not the end, of the whole creative enterprise. One of the skills the selling writer needs to develop is how to unleash the muse at the right time and then whip her material into shape for the greater needs of the story and the marketplace for that story.

That's why structure is so important. Structure enables story to get through to readers—you know, the ones who dish out the lettuce? That's why I call structure "translation software for your imagination." The no-structure mob may, every now and then (and almost always by accident) produce an "experimental" novel that gains some traction with critics (but rarely with readers). But the other 99 percent of such work fails to sell. I know many writers would love to be able to simply wear a beret, sit at Starbucks all day, and have whatever they write go out to the world and bring in abundant bank and critical accolades.

Not going to happen.

Meanwhile, more and more writers who have taken the time to study the craft are happily selling their books in this new, open marketplace we have.

Passion, Precision, and Productivity Make for Writing Success

To gain traction in this game, you would do well to consider the three Ps: passion, precision, and productivity.

PASSION. You find the kind of stories you are burning to tell. For me, it's usually contemporary suspense. I love reading it, so that's mostly what I write. But I also believe a writer can pick a genre and *learn* to love it the same way people in an arranged marriage sometimes love each other. The key is to find some emotional investment in what you write. But that's only the first step.

PRECISION. Eventually successful writers know precisely where the niche is for the books they write. They spend some time studying the market. That's how all the pulp writers and freelancers of the past made a living. Dean Koontz at one time wanted to be a comic novelist like Joseph Heller. But when his war farce didn't sell, he switched markets. He went all-in with thrillers. He's done pretty well at this.

PRODUCTIVITY. Finally, selling writers produce the words. These words won't be wasted. They will be making them better writers, because they have studied the craft and keep on studying.

The fun part of writing is being totally wild and writing in the zone. The work part of writing is shaping up the material so it has the best chance to connect with the market.

Therefore, writing friends, don't be lulled into thinking all you have to do each day is traipse through the tulips of your fertile imaginings, fingers following along on the keyboard, recording every jot and tittle of your genius. If you are writing for income as well as joy, write smart.

Write for the ages. Edit for the grocery store.

TEACH YOURSELF TO WRITE, THE JACK LONDON WAY

Once I made the decision to become a writer, I went after it with everything I had. There would be no going back, no surrender. In this I found myself feeling like one of my writing heroes, Jack London.

London was a self-taught writer who achieved success through an iron will and disciplined production. He also wrote one of the best novels about a writer, the largely autobiographical *Martin Eden*. There are long passages that get inside the writer's mind and heart, and also chronicle London's own efforts as a young man struggling to teach himself to write fiction. Let's take a look at a few of those.

Study, Don't Just Read, Successful Authors

[Martin] went farther in the matter. Reading the works of men who had arrived, he noted every result achieved by them, and worked out the tricks by which they had been achieved—the tricks of narrative, of exposition, of style, the points of view, the contrasts, the epigrams; and of all these he made lists for study. He did not ape. He sought principles. He drew up lists of effective and fetching mannerisms, till out of many such, culled from many writers, he was able to induce the general principle of mannerism, and, thus equipped, to cast about for new and original ones of his own, and to weigh and measure and appraise them properly.

When I started my writing journey I went to a local used bookstore and picked up an armload of thrillers by King, Koontz, Grisham, and others. As I read these books. I marked them up, wrote in the margins, talked to myself about what I was discovering, made notes about the techniques—sometimes on napkins or other scraps of paper. I still hang on to all of these notes.

Collect Examples of Style

In similar manner he collected lists of strong phrases, the phrases of living language, phrases that bit like acid and scorched like flame, or that glowed and were mellow and luscious in the midst of the arid desert of common speech. He sought always for the principle that lay behind and beneath. He wanted to know how the thing was done; after that he could do it for himself. He was not content with the fair face of beauty. He dissected beauty in his crowded little bedroom laboratory, where cooking smells alternated with the outer bedlam of the Silva tribe; and, having dissected and learned the anatomy of beauty, he was nearer being able to create beauty itself.

I have a notebook full of examples of great flights of style. I've copied, by hand, passages I've admired. The object was to get the sound of sentences in my head and expand my stylistic range.

You Can't Learn to Write Just by Writing

He was so made that he could work only with understanding. He could not work blindly, in the dark, ignorant of what he was producing and trusting to chance and the star of his genius that the effect produced should be right and fine. He had no patience with chance effects.

This resonates with me, because I've often heard the advice that you should shun craft study and just write. Like you should shun medical school and just perform surgery. As I said in the previous section, good writing should be a marriage between writing and the study of the craft.

Beware Pantsing

> He wanted to know why and how. His was deliberate creative genius, and, before he began a story or poem, the thing itself was already alive in his brain, with the end in sight and the means of realizing that end in his conscious possession. Otherwise the effort was doomed to failure.

Jack London knew what he wanted before he started to write. He knew the plot before he began to write, and he developed the tools to pull it off. Now, I love all you pantsers out there. I want you to succeed. Just beware the perils and trust that your left brain is actually part of your head, too. Give it a listen every once in awhile.

But Don't Choke Off Inspired Moments

> On the other hand, he appreciated the chance effects in words and phrases that came lightly and easily into his brain, and that later stood all tests of beauty and power and developed tremendous and incommunicable connotations. Before such he bowed down and marveled, knowing that they were beyond the deliberate creation of any man. And no matter how much he dissected beauty in search of the principles that underlie beauty and make beauty possible, he was aware, always, of the innermost mystery of beauty to which he did not penetrate and to which no man had ever penetrated.

There are times that something may "work," even if you don't know why. So go with it, try it, let that character or section of prose fly off your fingertips. Just be ready to "kill the darling" if enough people tell you it ain't working. I've reached for many a metaphor that my lovely wife has told me is more confusing than enlightening. She is almost always right about this.

Embrace the Wonder

> He knew full well ... that the mystery of beauty was no less than that of life—nay, more that the fibres of beauty and life were intertwisted, and that he himself was but a bit of the same nonunderstandable fabric, twisted of sunshine and star-dust and wonder.

The story of Martin Eden proceeds from this point to a tragic ending. I think it's because Martin failed to follow his sense of beauty to a source and instead succumbed to a meaningless Nietzschean void. That matter is best discussed in a classroom.

For our purposes, keep the magic alive in your writing. Don't you love being a writer? Doesn't it feel sometimes that you are made up of sunshine, stardust, and wonder? Yes, there are also times you feel like the tar on the bottom of a dockworker's boot, but you accept that as the price for feeling the other, don't you?

How are you teaching yourself to write?

PUT MORE STRINGS IN YOUR WRITING BOW

I'm a fan of the Parker novels by Donald Westlake (writing as Richard Stark). I've seen all the film versions, like *Point Blank* with Lee Marvin, *The Outfit* with Robert Duvall, and *Payback* with Mel Gibson.

Payback, a 1999 release, is particularly good. But I recently became aware that the director, Brian Helgeland, had the film taken away from him. His version did not test well, so a new third act was written under the eye of Gibson, who was one of the producers.

A few years ago, Helgeland was given permission to release his director's cut. I recently watched it. It is darker and perhaps truer to the feel of the novels. I do think, however, Mel and Paramount were correct. The 1999 version is more satisfying.

But I digress. The reason I'm mentioning this is that the director's cut has an interview with the late, great Westlake on the genesis of Richard Stark and the Parker novels.

Westlake was putting out one hardcover book a year under his own name. Wanting to make a living as a writer, he decided he needed "another string in his bow." He decided to try the paperback original market, which was geared mostly for a male audience in those days.

He wanted the books to be lean and dark. "Without adverbs," he said. "Stark."

That's how he came up with the last name for his pseudonym.

He chose Richard because he liked the iconic noir actor Richard Widmark.

That's how Richard Stark was born.

Then he needed a name for his character. He chose Parker. With a wry smile he said he wished he'd chosen another name, because he spent so much time trying to come up with other ways to say, "Parker parked the car."

In any event, his agent showed the first book, *The Hunter,* to Gold Medal, the leading paperback-originals publisher of the day. Rejected. So they tried Pocket Books. An editor with the wonderful name of Bucklin Moon liked it.

The original manuscript ended with Parker in jail. He did not, in other words, get away with it (*it* being the killing of some bad guys in order to get money owed him from a heist). Moon asked Westlake if he would consider changing the ending so he could make it a series, and if could he turn out three books a year.

Westlake jumped at the chance.

What happened over the next several years is that Richard Stark started selling better than Donald Westlake, which irked Westlake the author ... but pleased Westlake the guy who wanted to make a living.

And so Parker became one of the great characters of hard noir.

When self-publishing took off in 2008, I said it felt like the mass-market boom of the 1950s, where many literary authors, like Evan Hunter writing as Ed McBain or Gore Vidal writing as Edgar Box, made extra money.

So take a tip from the past: We can, like Westlake, have more strings in our bows, and self-publishing offers that opportunity. But unlike Westlake and writers of that era, we don't have to use a pseudonym. Independent publishing distinguishes brands by way of cover design, book description, and keyword categories. Writers can therefore gain fans in different categories, making some cross-pollination of fans not only possible, but probable. Readers have found me by way of my vigilante nun series and gone on to sample my historical novels. Imagine that!

Back when I started getting paid for writing, there was only one stream available for the professional scribe. Now there are three: traditional, independent, and a river made up of both.

And that's good news for writers of every stripe who love to write and who want to stretch and grow—and make some actual money.

Put more strings in your bow.

WRITING BOW EXERCISES

1. Name your three favorite genres to read.
2. What do you like about each one? What is it about that kind of storytelling that connects with you?
3. Pick one genre that you have not written much in. Write a scene (just make one up) in that genre.
4. Can you expand that into a short story (1,000–6,000 words)? Or a novelette (6,000–15,000)? How about a novella (15,000–40,000)?
5. Consider taking one month to write a completed work of any size in that genre. If you are ambitious, use November and NaNo WriMo to write a 50,000-word novel.

GOING DEEPER WITH YOUR FICTION

There is a lot more *pretty good* fiction out there than there used to be. With all of the teaching and conferences and blogs that have sprung up over the last twenty years, writers who care about the craft are more equipped than ever to raise the level of their game. So when I go to a conference and see manuscripts, they are generally of a higher quality than I saw back when I started on the circuit. Sure, you're always going to have manuscripts that are not ready for late night, let alone prime time, but I do think fiction writers in general are turning in more *competent* material.

That's a good thing. It's just not good enough. Because with so much content out there that is okay, a writer has to find ways to do *better* than okay in order to thrive. They have to find ways to go *deeper*.

When I say "deeper," I mean deeper for the reader. We want to weave a fictive dream, make it vivid, and stop doing things that jolt them out of the trance. That's one of the big reasons for studying the craft—learning to spot the "speed bumps" that jolt a reader, even a little bit, out of your dream.

Now, dreams are experienced emotionally and, only later, analyzed for meaning. It's the same with fiction. We want the readers to be emotionally engaged and, when the book is over, thinking about what a great ride it was.

So emotion is a big key to going deeper.

Something I emphasize in my workshops is what I call *crosscurrents of emotion*, where readers experience multiple emotions through a scene or character, and sometimes those emotions are conflicting.

The nice thing about this is readers do not pause to analyze the emotions. They feel them, and the more going on, the better. This makes for a novel they will call *awesome* or *memorable*, rather than merely *enjoyable*.

Crosscurrents of emotion are created in three ways.

Characters in Conflict

Show the characters experiencing conflicting emotions. Let's say a boy and girl meet, and they are attracted to one another. The boy is a vampire. He wants to kiss the girl but also to suck her blood. You could write that scene emphasizing only the emotion of love. Or only the horror of it. But if you have equally strong currents of bloodsucking lust and incipient romance, you get an almost exponential emotional deepening.

So how do you get at some of these deeper emotions in your fiction? Here are a few exercises I teach in workshops:

Chair Through the Window

Imagine that your lead character is in a nice living room with a big bay window. The window looks out on a lovely garden. There is a chair sitting by the piano. Your lead picks up the chair and throws it through the window. Now ask yourself why. What would make your character do that? It all depends on what kind of character you've been writing. But this surprising, shocking action is motivated by something. Brainstorm what that is until you find the motivation that strikes you in the gut.

Closet Search

The police come to where your character lives. They have a search warrant. In your character's closet is one thing that she never wants anyone to see, ever. What is that thing? What does that tell you about her inner life? Brainstorm that item until you find something fresh and, more important, disturbing.

Good Cop/Bad Cop

Now your character is sitting under the hot lights in an old 1940s film noir. There is a tough, cigar-smoking police detective who is haranguing your character, trying to force her to admit something, confess something. What is she trying to hide? When you find out what it is, the thing that she does not want to reveal to anyone, have her fight back. She won't talk to the bad cop. But she is sweating under those lights. Then the good cop steps in and tells the bad cop to leave the room. He is warm and understanding and your character trusts him. Now she makes her confession. What does she tell this man?

The Dickens

I love this one. Go forward in time twenty years from the end of your novel. If you've done a Civil War novel, go to 1885. If you've done a sci-fi novel set in 3156, go to 3176. You are now going to play reporter and interview your lead character. If your lead has died in the novel, talk to the ghost. This is called "The Dickens," because you are going to the future, like Scrooge did.

Sit down with your reporter's notepad and ask the lead these questions, similar to "How Should Characters Change?" in chapter three:

- Why did you have to go through all that (the events of the novel)?
- What did you learn about yourself?
- What did you learn about life?
- If you could give a message to today's audience, what would it be?
- What would your life have been like had you *not* experienced the novel? Is that the sort of life you would have preferred?

The Dickens may be done at any time, but it's especially effective when done after you've read your first draft for the first time.

Crosscurrents in Readers

You can do things to create crosscurrents of emotion in the readers themselves. One of the most powerful ways to do this is to give a villain a sympathy factor. As I've already mentioned, this is much more effective than the stereotypical, all-evil-all-the-time bad guy. Readers don't want to empathize with evil, and that's a good thing. But they also don't want to be manipulated. By giving them a fully rounded villain, you create conflicting emotions *inside the reader*.

The amazing thing is the readers won't dislike you for that. Instead, they will sense that the whole reading experience has done something to them on the inside. And you know what they'll do after that? Recommend your book to their friends! That's the secret to a career, ladies and gentlemen.

Tears in the Writer

Robert Frost said, "No tears in the writer, no tears in the reader." The meaning is obvious. Unless you, dear writer, are experiencing something emotionally as you write, your scene will have that much less "vibration" in it. Just as *joy* is evident when you are telling your tale well, so too is emotional vibrancy.

Remember the opening of *Romancing the Stone*? Romance writer Joan Wilder (Kathleen Turner) has headphones on, pumping music, as she types the last scene of her work in progress. And by the end of it, she's crying up a storm.

You need to experience some waterworks, too, as a writer. But you also need to experience *any* strong emotion as you write a scene.

How do you get there? You place your characters in real conflict. You get inside the viewpoint character's head. You call upon your own life to experience what that character is experiencing (this is a little exercise method actors call "sense memory").

Once you're there, write that scene for all it's worth. *Overwrite* it, in fact. You can always "pull back" on the intensity level when you revise.

In short, don't settle for good enough fiction. Push past the familiar and the easy and the okay. Get emotional!

THE PERILS OF PURE PANTSING

There are pansters. And then there are pure pantsers.

Pantsers (derived from the idiom "seat of the pants," as in performing an act solely by instinct) are those writers who do not plan (or plan very little) before they write. These folks love to frolic in the tulips of the imagination. "We get to fall in love with our words every day," they say. "We are intuitive. Don't rain your outlines on our parade!"

Okay, well, that's *one* approach to writing a book, and there is nothing sinful about it. I am not saying that this is in any way an invalid method of finishing a manuscript—so long as you recognize the hard work that must follow to shape a readable novel out of this mass of pantsed material. But to any writer or teacher who says writing this way is not only best, but easy, feed them this phrase: *Pants on fire!*

The "pure pantsers" are a more radical ilk. These are the ones who want to throw away all thought of *structure*, whether at the beginning or the end. They find structure formulaic and offensive to their artistic sensibilities. They stand on their tables and shout, *Off with the shackles of what's been taught all these years! Throw away the tools of the craft! We are the true writers around here! We laugh at you structurally imprisoned slaves! Join us!*

So let's have some plain talk about pantsing.

In *The Liar's Bible,* Lawrence Block recalls writing one of his Bernie Rhodenbarr mysteries. Larry wrote, and did so without an outline or even the thought of one, then looked up from his manuscript one day and observed:

> I had incidents. I had plot elements. I had characters in search of a story. But all manner of things were happening in my book and I didn't have the faintest idea what was going on. Why had a man named Onderdonk inveigled Bernie into appraising his library? What were hairs from a golden retriever doing in the cuffs of a corpse's pants? Who was the young woman Bernie ran into in the Kroll apartment, and how did she fit into what was going on? Who had stolen Carolyn's cat, and how, and why? What connected the Mondrian in Onderdonk's apartment, which someone else had stolen, with the one in the Hewlett Museum, which Bernie was supposed to steal in order to ransom the cat? If I couldn't answer any of these questions, who could? And if nobody could, how could I keep on writing the book? ...
>
> ... For a time I persisted, telling myself to Trust The Process, and feeling all the while like a Christian Scientist with appendicitis. Then,

with 175 pages written and a maximum of 75 left in which to Wrap Things Up, I stopped writing and threw up my hands. And my lunch.

All pantsers face this at some point. They have to wade into that mass of verbiage and excreta and figure out what's good, what's dreck, what fits, what doesn't, and where the story is going and how to help it get there. But if they have been told to "forget about structure," they are lost at sea with no navigation tools in a leaky boat.

Sometimes I have to fire up my rescue dinghy and motor out there with a life jacket.

I once consulted with a #1 *New York Times* best-selling author. She called on me because she's a fan of *Plot & Structure* and needed help getting a novel idea into shape. The book was fighting her, as she put it. The structure felt off and she had pages due to her publisher.

So we sat down for three hours and hashed it out. It was easy duty for me because she understands structure. She's studied it. She's used it. She knows it.

So I helped her push her protagonist through the first Doorway of No Return, into Act II, in a much stronger way. There was a sub-plot that wasn't working, so we dug deeper into the characters and their motivations, and that solved it.

And since this was the first book in a series, we looked ahead to future books and planted important material in this one.

Her book has since been published and hit the *New York Times* Bestseller list.

After that meeting I had another consultation, this time with a new writer. He has a pantser's mind, and it shows. He writes pages and pages, and his imagination soars ... but he goes off on tangents. Ideas burst out of him, but he has no idea what to do with them, how to form them into a coherent story. When I sat down with him, he said, with obvious frustration, "I know I can write, but I don't know where this story is going!"

So I walked him through some key questions, based on what I call signpost scenes. These scenes are critical to your story, and you need to be writing (even pantsing!) toward them as you go. After I prodded him with a few "What ifs," he started to get it. He began to see the structure of the whole plot laid out in his mind. He was excited. He could feel the strength that structure gave him, and the direction: He now knows what kind of scenes to write so that they are organic and related to the plot. He is not just spinning his scribal wheels.

So, I am *not* telling you to stop pantsing your way through a manuscript. I *am* telling you that at some point you have to face structure because if you don't, you're going to end up with a novel that doesn't sell, except by accident. (Yes, accidents happen, but that's no way to build a career.)

Sure, there are some writers who say they don't ever think about structure and they do just fine. I believe about 10 percent of them. These, I believe, are the lucky ones. They can intuit their way to a novel that works. Maybe even on the first draft (you can choose to hate Lee Child at this point). But the structure is always there, even if they don't plan for it. They've simply got it in their writing bones.

But the overwhelming majority of authors need to study and utilize structure and technique. I recall a sad story about a talented writer (his prose was superb) who inked a deal for a three-book thriller series. The first book came out and bombed, and as a consequence, the big publisher let the other two "die on the vine."

I read that first book and my heart just sank for the guy, because his structure was off. He made some obvious craft mistakes up front which resulted in a dull first act (which you really want to avoid in the thriller genre). I wish I could have been his editor, because with a little help, so much of the trouble could have been avoided.

Here's the key to everything: You must put your original voice, vision, style, spice, characters, love, and passion into a story that, structurally, *helps readers feel what you want them to feel.*

That's what the craft of structure is about. It's not to limit you, the artist. It's to set free your story so an actual audience can enjoy it.

So go ahead and pants your way through a first draft if you like. But after that, put on bib overalls and get your tools out and start working on the structure.

You may wish to ignore this advice. You may seek to pitch a tent in Occupy Storytelling Park, grow a beard, and rail at the passing pedestrians. But understand this: Several of these pedestrians will be writers who know structure and are on their way to the bank to cash their checks.

FIRST BE A STORYTELLER

I was a student at U.C. Santa Barbara, one of the best film studies programs in the country, during the golden age of American movies. The 1970s saw an explosion of great independent films and directors, many of whom were picked up by major studios. Our intimate band of film majors had the opportunity to talk with exciting new directors like Martin Scorsese, Robert Altman, Lina Wertmuller, and Alan Rudolph.

But this was also the time when many of the great directors of the past were still alive, and they also came up for a visit. I got to chat with film giants like King Vidor, Rouben Mamoulian, and one of my all-time favorite directors, Frank Capra. Also, I met the legendary cinematographer James Wong Howe. Heady times indeed!

Film studies at that time were heavily into the "auteur theory," which came to us from the French critics. This theory embraced directors with a marked style that was evident in their movies. You can always tell a film by Welles, Hitchcock, Josef von Sternberg, Chaplin, Keaton, and so on. Visual and thematic consistency are the marks of the auteur.

Over the years, though, I have come to appreciate a director who is usually left off the list of the greats. I believe he belongs near the top, and for reasons auteur theorists often reject. He belongs simply because he may be the best storyteller of them all.

William Wyler (1902–1981) was a studio director who refused to get tied down to one genre (usually an auteur requirement). All he did was tell one mesmerizing story after another. If you step back and look at his output, you have to shake your head in wonder. Here are just a few of his titles:

Dodsworth
Jezebel
Wuthering Heights
The Little Foxes
Mrs. Miniver
The Heiress

Classics, all. But look at what else is on his list:

A great Western, *The Big Country*. A great musical, *Funny Girl*. The greatest biblical epic of the all, *Ben-Hur*. *Roman Holiday* (a romance). *The Desperate Hours* (suspense). *Friendly Persuasion* (Americana).

And right in the middle, what I consider to be the greatest film ever produced in America, *The Best Years of Our Lives*. I rewatched it recently with my family and, once again, was knocked senseless by it. The mark of a classic is that it gets better every time you see it. *Best Years* is such a film.

So what was it about Wyler? He wasn't hyperactive with his camera work (a lesson many of today's filmmakers could benefit from). Why not? *Because he didn't want to get in the way of the story.* Instead, what you see in a Wyler film is a respect for the script, a superb direction of actors, and shots that are framed to *tell* the story, not to shout out what a great director he is—even though those very virtues made him great.

What's the lesson here for writers? Those who really make a dent, be it in the traditional world, independent, or "blended," are all about *story*. When I have to choose between a novel that has beautiful style but a dull story and a novel that has a killer plot with serviceable writing, I'll choose the latter every time.

What really rocks for me is when a great plot meets with a style that has what John D. MacDonald called "unobtrusive poetry." That's how I would describe William Wyler's films.

Above all, tell a great story. Give us characters we can't resist, even the bad ones. Give us "death stakes." Give us twists, turns, and cliff-hangers. Give us heart.

Don't stress about style. Get excited about the tale. That's the key to the elusive concept of "voice." If readers get just as excited about your story as you are, you've done it. You've clanged the bell, nabbed the brass ring, knocked a grand slam over the green monster at Fenway.

And if you've never seen *The Best Years of Our Lives,* get it on DVD or stream it, and schedule a good three-hour stretch to watch it without interruption. You'll marvel at the genius of William Wyler, storyteller.

STORY. DAMMIT, STORY!

In his introduction to Stephen King's *Night Shift,* John D. MacDonald explains what it takes to become a successful writer. Diligence, a love of words, and empathy for people are three big factors. But he sums up the primary element this way: "Story. Dammit, story!"

And what is story? It is, says MacDonald, "something happening to somebody you have been led to care about."

Something happening is the soil in which plot is planted, watered, and harvested for glorious consumption by the reader. Without it, the reading experience can quickly become a dry biscuit, with no butter or honey in sight.

Mind you, there are readers who like dry biscuits. Just not very many.

MacDonald reminds us that without the "something happening," you do not have a story at all. What you have is a collection of words that may at times fly but ultimately ends up frustrating more than it entertains.

I thought of MacDonald's essay when I came across an amusing (at least to me) letter that had been written to James Joyce about his novel *Ulysses.* I found it amusing because the letter was penned by no less a luminary than Carl Jung, one of the giants of twentieth century psychology.

Here, in part, is what Jung wrote to Joyce:

> I had an uncle whose thinking was always to the point. One day he stopped me on the street and asked, "Do you know how the devil tortures the souls in hell?" When I said no, he declared, "He keeps them waiting." And with that he walked away. This remark occurred to me when I was ploughing through *Ulysses* for the first time. Every sentence raises an expectation which is not fulfilled; finally, out of sheer resignation, you come to expect nothing any longer. Then, bit by bit, again to your horror, it dawns upon you that in all truth you have hit the nail on the head. It is actual fact that nothing happens and nothing comes of it, and yet a secret expectation at war with hopeless resignation drags the reader from page to page ... You read and read and read and you pretend to understand what you read. Occasionally you drop through an air pocket into another sentence, but when once the proper degree of resignation has been reached you accustom yourself to anything. So I, too, read to page one hundred and thirty-five with despair in my heart, falling asleep twice on the way ... Nothing comes to meet the reader, everything turns away from him, leaving him gaping after it. The book is always up and away, dissatisfied with itself, ironic, sardonic, virulent, contemptuous, sad, despairing, and bitter ...

Now, I'm no Joyce scholar, and I'm sure there are champions of *Ulysses* who might want to argue with Jung and maybe kick him in the id, but I think he speaks for the majority of those who made an attempt at reading the novel and felt that "nothing came to meet them."

I felt a bit of the same about the movie *Cake,* starring Jennifer Aniston. When the Oscar nominations came out that year, it was said that Aniston was "snubbed" by not getting a nod. I entirely agree. Aniston is brilliant in this dramatic turn.

The problem the voters had, I think, is that the film feels more like a series of disconnected scenes than a coherently designed, three-act story. The effect is that after about thirty minutes the film begins to drag, even though Aniston is acting up a storm. Good acting is not enough to make a story just as beautiful prose is not enough to make a novel.

Years ago a certain writing instructor taught popular workshops on freeing up the mind and letting the words flow. The workshops were good as far as they went, for this instructor taught nothing about plot or structure. Finally the day came when the instructor wrote a novel. It was highly anticipated, but ultimately tanked with critics and buyers. And me. As I suspected, there were passages of great beauty and lyricism, but there was no compelling plot. No 'something happening to someone we have been led to care about."

Of course, when beautiful prose meets a compelling character, and things do happen in a structured flow, you've got everything going for you. But prose should be the servant, not the master, of your tale.

Let me suggest an exercise. Watch *Casablanca*. Pause the film every ten minutes or so, and ask yourself:

1. What is happening?
2. Why do I care about Rick? (i.e., what does he *do* that makes him a character worth watching?)
3. Why do I want to keep watching?

You can analyze any book or film in this way, and it will be a highly instructive and worthwhile pursuit.

Also, consider putting this little sign by your computer:

STORY. DAMMIT, STORY!

LOVE, LOSS, AND EMOTION IN OUR WRITING

Her name was Susan and we were in the third grade. I saw her for the first time on the playground. She had blonde hair that was almost white, and eyes as blue as a slice of sky laid atop God's light table.

She looked at me and I felt actual heat in my chest.

Remember that scene in *The Godfather* where Michael Corleone, hiding out in Sicily, sees Appolonia for the first time? His two friends notice the look on his face and tell him, "I think you got hit by the thunder bolt!"

When it happens to us at eight years old, we don't exactly have a metaphor for it, but that's what it was—the thunder bolt. Love at first sight!

I remember the ache I felt the rest of the day. My life had changed, divided into two periods (admittedly of not too lengthy duration)— before Susan and after Susan.

Now what? Having no experience with love, I wondered what the next step was supposed to be. How did love work itself out when your mom was packing your lunches and your allowance was twenty-five cents a week?

I'd seen *The Adventures of Robin Hood* with Errol Flynn. He climbed up the vines to Maid Marian's balcony. Was that a plan? Not in Woodland Hills, California, a suburb of mostly one-story ranch-style homes. Clearly the balcony strategy was out.

I had also seen the 1938 version of *Tom Sawyer* (I was getting most of my life lessons from movies and Classics Illustrated comic books) and was enamored with his love for Becky Thatcher. And what had Tom done to impress Becky? Why, he showed off, of course.

There was my answer. I would show off in front of Susan.

What was I good at? Kick ball. Athletic prowess would be my ticket into Susan's heart. So out on the playground I made my voice loud and clear when I came up for my kicks. Susan was usually nearby playing four square.

And every now and then we'd make eye contact. That's when I'd kick that stupid ball all the way to the fence.

Yet I was shy, afraid to talk to her directly. I mean, what was I going to say? *Want to see my baseball cards, baby? How about joining me for a Jell-O at lunch? Hey, that nurse's office is really something, isn't it?*

Flummoxed, I thought of Susan for weeks without ever exchanging a word with her. She had no problem with that, it seemed. But she knew I liked her. The rumor mill at school was a fast and efficient communication system. Which only made me more embarrassed.

I considered running away and joining the circus, but my parents were against it.

Then one day circumstances coalesced and the stars aligned.

School was out and kids were heading for the gate to walk home or get picked up. I usually went out the front gate. Susan went out the back, and this day I fell in with that company and quickened my pace to get next to her. Heart pounding, I said something suave like, "Hi." I don't recall that she said anything, but at once I found we were side by side, walking down the street.

I started talking about our teacher, Mr. McMahon, who was tall and imposing and, to third graders, seemed somewhat mean (thus in hallways and safely out on the playground, we referred to him, in whispered tones, as "Mr. McMonster").

Susan said nothing. I started to get more confident. Maybe, just maybe, she was interested in what I had to say. And maybe, just maybe, oh hope of all hopes, she actually liked me back.

All of that showing off was about to pay dividends!

And then came one of those moments you never forget, that burn into your memory banks with a searing, permanent heat. Susan turned to me and spoke for the first time. And this is what she said:

"Just because I'm walking with you doesn't mean you're my *boyfriend.*"

It was the way she said *boyfriend* that did it. It dripped with derision and perhaps a bit of mockery. If I could have found a gopher hole, I would have dived in, hoping for a giant subterranean rodent to eat me up and end my shame.

This all happened fifty years ago, yet I can still see it, hear it, and feel it as if it were last week.

Is that not why some of us are writers? To create scenes that burn like that, with vividness and emotion, rendering life's moments in such a way as to let others experience them? To share some of our own past in a meaningful way? Like first love. We never forget it. And first rejection—it never goes away.

I want my fiction to create memorable moments for my readers and thus, even if it's only in some small way, help them through this cockeyed existence. Even if it's "only entertainment," that's something I think we need. "In a world of so much pain and fear and cruelty," writes Dean Koontz in *How to Write Best Selling Fiction*, "it is noble to provide a few hours of escape." And the way into that escapism is to create emotional moments that seem real and vibrant and even life altering. We tap into that in our writing by going back to our own moments and translating them for fictional purposes.

Thus Susan was part of my becoming who I am and how I write.

So Susan, my first love, wherever you are, thank you. Maybe I wasn't your *boyfriend*, but you taught me what it's like to love and lose. I can use that. All of life is material!

I hope you're well. I hope you've found true and lasting love, like I have. I want you to know I hold you no ill will.

But always remember this: I'm still the best kick ball player you ever saw.

LOVE AND LOSS EXERCISES

1. Journal, in detail, about a great love and great loss in your life.
2. Implant similar emotions in your lead character.
3. Journal about other deep emotions you've experienced. Keep these as character fodder for future projects.

WRITE YOUR TRUTH

On a cool April night in 1950, a young actor got the chance to do a scene in the Actor's Studio, in front of the legendary Lee Strasberg. This was the Valhalla of all up-and-coming actors in New York. It wasn't easy to get a scene here, let alone be invited to join.

The scene called for this young actor to portray a soldier dying of gangrene. When the actor finished, Strasberg proceeded to tell him he had not sufficiently portrayed the pain of someone dying of this condition.

The actor interrupted him. He said that he, Strasberg, was the one who was misinformed. You see, this actor had been a Marine in combat during World War II and had seen soldiers dying of gangrene. He knew that in the final stages they felt no pain at all.

Furious at being contradicted in front of the class, Strasberg told the actor to leave and never return. The actor responded with a two-word exit line before storming off.

This young actor's name was Lee Marvin. From that point on, he would infuse his acting jobs with whatever truth was inside him. And what was inside him was a volcano.

Growing up, Marvin had attention deficit disorder and dyslexia in a time when no one really knew how to deal with them. More discipline was the only prescription at the time. No wonder Marvin hated school and was constantly in trouble. He was always fighting. Once, as a teenager in a boarding school that his parents sent him to in desperation, his roommate threw some trash out the window. Marvin told him that was a stupid thing to do. The roommate called him a son of a bitch. Marvin later recalled, "I said, 'Call me that again and I'll throw you out the window.' He called me it again and I threw him out the window. So, they kicked me out of school."

With fighting such a constant in his life, it should be no surprise that, at age seventeen, Lee Marvin joined the Marines just after the attack on Pearl Harbor.

It was a right fit for him, and he toughed out his training and eventually shipped out for action in the South Pacific. But what he saw there was not the glamour of war often depicted in the movies. He saw life-altering horror. He was a sniper with many kills. He also engaged in hand-to-hand combat, wiped out machine gun nests, and was almost killed on several occasions. When a Japanese soldier came at his face with a bayonet, Marvin took it away and bayoneted the soldier "all the way to the gun barrel ..."

A climactic battle in Saipan resulted in 80 percent casualties in Marvin's unit. Marvin was wounded and ended up in a hospital. He was twenty-one years old.

After the war, Marvin dealt with post-traumatic stress disorder, alcoholism, and a four-pack-a-day cigarette habit for the rest of his life.

But American men of that era were expected to "soldier on" in life, and that's what Marvin did. Like so many returning vets, he had a hard time finding a viable career. He spent time digging ditches and hand-threading pipes. And drinking.

Then one morning in 1946, Marvin found himself sleeping off a drunken stupor in a public park in Woodstock, New York. A Red Cross nurse woke him up and started talking about community service. Next thing he knew he was involved in a local Red Cross benefit at the town hall, a production entitled (appropriately) "Ten Nights in a Barroom."

He caught the acting bug. He did what most actors did in those days, pounding the pavement in New York. He got some work, told Lee Strasberg off, and later headed to Hollywood where he heard there was money. He started landing small roles and then turned up on an early *Dragnet* episode. Jack Webb, star and producer of the cop show, was so impressed with Marvin's performance that he made sure influential people around town saw it.

Marvin's breakout role was Larry Vance, a mob strong arm in Fritz Lang's *The Big Heat*. In a chilling moment that made movie history, Larry gets mad at his girlfriend, played by Gloria Graham. She's been yapping to a cop. He throws a pot of scalding coffee in her face. Marvin became a steady movie heavy after that, with an occasional touchdown in comedy.

He did a TV series, *M Squad*. He did it for the money and in order to increase his name recognition. But he didn't like it. Later he said, "Creatively, an actor is limited in TV. The medium is great for pushing goods. Sell the product, that's the goal ... But, I'm not interested in pushing the products; I'm interested in Lee Marvin, and where he's going as an actor."

We writers need to ask ourselves the same thing. Are we just trying to push a product, or do we have somewhere we want to go as a writer? Are we playing it safe? Or is there a truth we have that is burning to get out?

When Marvin was cast as the drunken gunfighter in *Cat Ballou* (1965), no one thought the movie or the role would do that much. But it became a surprise hit, and Marvin's hilarious performance (given reality by his own struggle with the bottle) ended up winning him an Academy Award for Best Actor of the Year.

And that, in turn, rocketed Marvin into star status. After that he took on some iconic roles, including the tough major in *The Dirty Dozen* and the remorseless thief bent on revenge in *Point Blank*.

But I think my favorite Marvin performance is in the underappreciated Western, *Monte Walsh* (1970). It's an elegiac tribute to a cowboy in the fading West who refuses to give in. In a way, it sums up what the actor was all about. There's a point in the film when Walsh is offered a part in a Wild West show, but he'd have to dress up in gaudy duds and put on a false front. Despite the money, comfort, and security this would offer him, he refuses, saying, "I ain't spittin' on my whole life."

Walsh lived his life with purpose and truth he was willing to stand up for.

When you can get that quality into your art—acting, fiction, painting, song—you are leaving behind something more than product pushing.

What kind of artist do you want to be?

Chapter 7

WRITE WITH EFFICIENCY

Part of becoming a successful writer—and one who develops a healthy writing life—is learning to write with efficiency. Manage time, figure out those things that may scuttle your writing and then ... gasp ... don't do those things! This section covers several of these issues.

ENTERTAIN YOUR READER

"I have been writing for nineteen years and I have been successful probably because I have always realized that I knew nothing about writing, and have merely tried to tell an interesting story entertainingly."

So wrote Edgar Rice Burroughs in an article for *Writer's Digest* in 1930. I love the up-front honesty of the statement. It resonates with me because the first "real" book I read all the way through was *Tarzan of the Apes*. I still remember the feeling of being gripped by a story that wouldn't let me go. When I put the book down, I knew I wanted to do the same thing someday, to write a book that gripped the reader from start to finish.

I can even remember being pulled in so deep that I put everything else aside—playing outside, watching television, riding my bike to the candy store—just so I could finish that book!

As the saying goes, "That's entertainment!" But you'll always find a discussion going on somewhere about the merits of "entertaining" or "commercial" fiction versus "literary" fiction or "art." I find these discussions to be increasingly irrelevant.

Dickens, Dumas, Dostoevsky—The D Boys—all wrote great artistic works for a popular audience. Fitzgerald and Thomas

Wolfe certainly desired a wide readership. In the pulps, Chandler and Hammett and Dorothy Hughes had the readers, but also said meaningful things about the mean streets and the human condition.

None of these authors wrote without the desire for financial return. As Samuel Johnson so eloquently put it, "No man but a blockhead ever wrote, except for money."

Out on the edges, sure, you have the solo artist who doesn't give a rip what others think. And so he creates experimental pieces that don't sell, except on rare lightning-strike occasions.

On the other side of this divide are those who "write" monster porn (yes, it really exists) and somehow find people willing to pay for it.

But in the great in-between are those who want to entertain an audience. For some, entertaining is enough. Others want to add a little more heft to their style or theme, and that's a good thing. Still others want to transcend genre conventions and reach for the stars. I especially like that.

Tell a great story, no matter your genre or style. This is what readers reward. As Burroughs concluded in that *Writer's Digest* article:

> I have felt that it was a duty to those people who bought my books that I should give them the very best within me. I have no illusions as to the literary value of what I did give them, but I have the satisfaction of knowing that I gave them the best that my ability permitted.

ENTERTAINMENT EXERCISES

1. Write out a vision statement for yourself as a writer. What do you want to write, and how do you want the marketplace to view your output?
2. How do you feel about "commercial" fiction? Is there something holding you back from the notion of entertaining readers? Where does that come from?
3. How can you best serve readers with your writing? Explain.

YOUR NOVEL'S GREATEST DANGER

As I write this, a certain TV show is about to be cancelled. Not exactly headline worthy, I know. Happens all the time. Only this time it was a series I was trying to get into, mainly because I've liked the lead actor in the past.

The ratings were okay for the opener but gradually declined. I was one of those decliners. After four episodes I stopped watching.

The show has a unique setting, a cast of beautiful people, and an ongoing criminal investigation. What went wrong?

I'll tell you what went wrong: *I just did not care about any of the characters.*

I didn't care who was trying to cheat whom. I didn't care who was hopping into whose bed. I didn't care who made money, lost money, was rich or poor or desperate or in love.

On the surface—and this must have impressed the network suits—the show had "everything." Glam, glitz, beefcake, cheesecake, a star. But after four hour-long episodes there was not a single character I bonded with.

Which, dear writer, is the greatest danger to your own novel.

You simply must connect reader with character—and right out of the gate, too.

How? By knowing that this is all a function of two essential dynamics, which are ... wait for it ... plot and character.

Wow, earth shattering!

Ah, but so often missed because *one is often emphasized at the expense of the other.*

Character alone won't do it. If it did, maybe I'd be able to get through more than twenty pages of *A Confederacy of Dunces* (I've tried three times and never made it).

Plot alone doesn't do it, because events have to matter to a character who matters to the reader.

While there are many techniques professional fiction writers utilize to make a character someone we care about, for now I want to suggest a single, powerful question you should ask about all your main characters.

You need to set yourself up for this, because it's a question not to be tossed out lightly.

So find a comfy spot. I like to use a corner table at my local coffee palace.

Have a notepad ready.

Spend ten minutes thinking about anything except your novel. Observe people, read some news or a blog.

Next, turn yourself (as much as possible) into a fully objective reader who is considering buying your book.

Here comes the question:

If I were at a party and someone told me about this character, what she's like and what has happened to her, would I want to spend two hours listening to her tell her story?

Be merciless in your answer. Write down the exact reasons you would want to hear more. If you don't come up with good ones, you've got work to do.

If someone described to me a selfish, flirty Southern belle, I wouldn't want to spend two seconds with her. But if that person also told me that this particular Southern belle is the only one in her family with the grit and guts to save her home during and after the Civil War, I think I'd want to hear more.

If someone told me about an unsure FBI trainee who came from poor circumstances, I'd be mildly interested. But make her the only person in the entire bureau who can get the most devious, intelligent, and malevolent murderer in the annals of crime to talk and I'm down for the whole story.

PIs are a dime a dozen. But if it's Philip Marlowe narrating, I want that two hours just to listen to how he describes all the twists and turns.

> It was a blonde. A blonde to make a bishop kick a hole in a stained-glass window.
>
> She gave me a smile I could feel in my hip pocket.

> There was a desert wind blowing that night. It was one of those hot dry Santa Anas that come down through the mountain passes and curl your hair and make your nerves jump and your skin itch. On nights like that every booze party ends in a fight. Meek little wives feel the edge of the carving knife and study their husbands' necks.

You have your assignment. Would you, as a perfect stranger, feel compelled to listen to the story your main character wants to tell?

If not, make it so.

If so, make it *more* so!

THE TEN COMMANDMENTS FOR WRITING FAILURE

Mr. Donald Keough, who died at the age of eighty-eight, was, for a time, the number-two man at Coca-Cola. This was during an era called the "Cola wars." Keough's job was to beat back the challenge of Pepsi, which was winning the younger set while Coke was out there trying to teach the world to sing in perfect harmony.

Keough was also the mastermind of one of the worst product blunders in history.

The original formula Coke (at least the one that came after they took the cocaine out of it) was, and is, the best-tasting cola ever. It was Fred Astaire to Pepsi's journeyman hoofer. It was Spencer Tracy to Pepsi's high school senior starring in the school production of *Our Town*.

But for some unknown reason—probably due to overpaid consultants—Keough decided to change the formula, and New Coke was born. With great fanfare, they rolled it out. And the country responded with a loud, collective *yechh!*

The pushback was so passionate that only ten weeks later they brought the old formula back, calling it "Classic Coke."

And sales boomed. The controversy became national news. The publicity turned out to be priceless.

Some cynics suggested the whole thing had been planned. If so, it was brilliant. But when asked Keough said, "We're not that dumb and not that smart."

Later on, with a bit of self-deprecatory wisdom, Mr. Keough wrote a book called *The Ten Commandments for Business Failure.* I thought they might also apply to writers, especially now that self-publishing is a viable business option for the "authorpreneur." Let's have a look.

1. Quit Taking Risks

Resting on your laurels. Mailing it in. Doing the same old, same old. Maybe that works for a few traditionally published and best-selling authors, but for the true writer, the one who wants to honor the craft and get better, risk taking is part of the plan. Take risks in characterization, plot, style, and theme. Risks, in turn, bring a certain excitement to the writing. And you know what? *Readers can sense that you're excited.* That makes your writing more appealing.

2. Be Inflexible

'Flexibility," writes Keough, "is a continual, deeply thoughtful process of examining situations and when warranted, quickly adapting to changing circumstances." These days, every writer, no matter who butters their bread (i.e., traditional, self) needs to be aware of process, changes in the marketplace and distribution channels, and quality improvements.

3. Isolate Yourself

Success in business means being in touch with both workers and customers. A good manager is one who walks around and knows what's going on in the building and in the satellite offices.

Writers, who by the very nature of the work spend most of their time alone, need to know how to nurture a fan base, work social media wisely, grow an e-mail list and, if contracted with a traditional house, schmooze a little with the increasingly nervous staff therein.

4. Assume Infallibility

You want to fail at this game? Then put a chip on your shoulder and always blame somebody else. Your critique group is a great place to start. Tell them you've forgotten more about writing than they'll ever know. Reject editors' notes. Then rail at the marketplace when your books don't sell. Do anything but admit you have weaknesses that need to be addressed.

5. Play the Game Close to the Foul Line

What Keough means by this is that cheating, even a little, will eventually catch up with you. In recent years we've seen instances of plagiarism and sockpuppetry snag writers and impact careers. Trust is built up over time but can be lost in an instant. Just ask Brian Williams.

6. Don't Take Time to Think

The saying in business is "data drives decisions." You have to stop doing things that don't lead to profit and do more of the things that do—which is why traditional publishing companies drop authors who aren't selling enough books. If you are a midlist writer who has been dropped, maybe it is time to think about turning your attention toward independent publishing.

When I was running a small business, I took time each week for "thinking, planning, and studying." What I learned, I put into practice. I stopped doing anything that did not give a good return on my investment of time and energy.

7. Put All Your Faith in Experts and Outside Consultants

Writers, more than ever, need to take responsibility for their own careers, no matter what side of the walls of the Forbidden City of Publishing they're on. You cannot simply hand everything over to an agent or publisher. You have to know what questions to ask and what terms to refuse. For example, you have to know how to limit a noncompete clause and define "out of print" in a way that is meaningful and fair (hint: it should be based on royalties earned, not on copies sold).

If you self-publish, the worst thing you can do is give some outfit thousands of dollars to get your book out there, and then thousands more for them to "market" your book. You need to know how to do this yourself. There are many resources, books, and blogs, that teach the basics of self-publishing.

8. Love Your Bureaucracy

In business, the bigger the organization the harder it is to move. Traditional publishing has been living this challenge for the past several years. Why only recently? Because when digital publishing took off sometime in between 2008 and 2009, the main reaction of the major publishing houses was to see it as a blip, nothing to worry about. They had their comfy bureaucracies.

Oops. Now we see all the changes that have been happening inside the Forbidden City, from the cutting of editorial staff, to tussles with Amazon, to new direct-to-consumer programs. It's been a difficult transition period that's still going on.

The independent writer, on the other hand, can move quickly but can also fall in love with systems that aren't ultimately helpful. For example, if you're spending 80 percent of your time on social media and 20 percent on your writing, you're actually heading backwards.

9. Send Mixed Messages

In business they say, "The main thing is to keep the main thing the main thing." As a writer, your main thing is to tell great stories. If you also want to be a bad-boy blogger or a mouthpiece for some political persuasion, just know that readers will have mixed reactions. If that doesn't bother you, fine. Just be intentional about it.

I consider myself a writer first and a teacher of writing second. What I do in my writing and in social media and on my blog, is consistent with those two things. That doesn't mean I won't share the occasional opinion in this book, but I keep most everything consistent with those two roles.

10. Be Afraid of the Future

Oh, this is major. For 150 years the publishing industry has operated one way. It had a settled distribution system and there were plenty of bookstores for their stock. All that has changed in a flash, leaving agents, editors, and trade-based writers wondering how this is all going to shake out. To which I provide the answer: No one knows.

The successful writer keeps writing and doesn't let anxiety freeze up his flying fingers. Keep writing, keep trying to get better.

Keough finishes his book with a bonus commandment:

11. Lose Your Passion for Work, for Life

You've got to find ways to keep the joy in your writing life. That doesn't mean it'll always be unicorns and rainbows. A lot of the time it's tar pits and tsetse flies. But an inner core of love for what you do, and hopes for what you can achieve, will keep the fire burning.

When the flame begins to dim, take a couple of days to relax, regroup, rethink. And reread. Take a few of your favorite novels off the shelf (or off your e-reader) and read a few chapters. Get caught up again in the romance of great storytelling. Soon enough you'll be itching to get back to the keyboard.

So here's a command: Write your best scene ever. When you're done, pour yourself a Coke ... the *real* thing. Once in a blue moon, the calories won't hurt you!

THE TEN CHARACTERISTICS OF HIGHLY EFFECTIVE WRITERS

Management experts are fond of lists of characteristics of successful executives, entrepreneurs, even companies. These lists distill the wisdom of observations made over the course of time. In the same way, after years of writers conferences and workshops, I've made note of several marks of the effective writer. Here is my top ten.

1. Desire

If you want to make it as a writer—and by "make it," I mean achieve a degree of success that involves monetary gain as well as fulfilling work—you have to want it. Not mildly. As Phyllis Whitney put it, "you must want it *enough*. Enough to take all the rejections, enough to pay the price of disappointment and discouragement while you are learning. Like any other artist, you must learn your craft—then you can add all the genius you like."

Is writing something you can imagine not doing? If so, then don't do it.

Lawrence Block once said, "If you want to write fiction, the best thing you can do is take two aspirins, lie down in a dark room, and wait for the feeling to pass. If it persists, you probably ought to write a novel."

Check your gut, your heart, and your head. If the three of them line up and tell you to write, then do it.

2. Perseverance

Your brother-in-law tells you to forget it, that you're not good enough to be a writer. He says there are just too many of them out there and your chances of making it are about the same as you becoming the opening act of the Justin Bieber Sprung from Jail concert, tell him to kindly take a powder and check back in ten years.

> "Don't quit. It's very easy to quit during the first ten years."
>
> **—ANDRE DUBUS**

3. Discipline

Okay, you have the desire to write. I had the desire to play college basketball. So I couldn't sit on my can and drink Corona all day, then show up for the first day of practice. I had to give things up and work hard, every day.

There is one discipline that rules them all, like that ring in that story, the one with the little guys with furry feet. Your one discipline is to *produce words.*

I'm talking about a quota.

And no, you can't get out of it.

Over the recent past I've heard a few voices of protest to this idea. Nah, you don't have to stick to a quota. It's too onerous. It'll suck the life out of you. You're an artist, after all. You don't have to be disciplined! Just be in love!

Yeah, love. Like you want to ask out the girl of your dreams, but you don't want to take a shower, wash your clothes, or clean up your apartment. It's love!

Listen, the discipline of writing even when you don't feel like it is the mark of the pro. Pro, as in someone who gets money for his work. If you want to make money, produce the words.

Here's what I advise in my workshops.

Look at your normal weekly schedule. See how much time you have to devote to writing. Determine how many words you can comfortably write in one average week.

Now, up that by 10 percent. You need to learn the discipline of stretching.

That's your weekly quota.

Divide that into days. Try to make that daily word count, but if you miss a day, don't sweat it. Make it up on the other days.

Keep track of your daily totals on a spreadsheet. Set up a formula to add up your words per day and per week.

I mean it. I've been doing this for over ten years. I can tell you how many words I wrote on any given project on any day in any of those years. I can tell you how many total words per year I wrote.

Oh, yes, and take one day off per week from writing. A writing Sabbath. Even God took a day of rest. Doing so recharges your batteries, and batteries are what you need to write that quota each week.

4. Craft Study

I've also heard a few squeaky voices chirping that you don't need to learn (indeed, some even say you can't learn) the rules of craft. They don't like rules. They would rather hang out with the writers who don't write to a quota and pretend it's all going to come flowing naturally, like an oil strike (without drilling, of course).

Some hate the idea that anyone would even suggest there are 'rules." Not for artists! They link arms and sing, "Rebels are we! Born to be free! Just like the fish in the sea!"

There used to be a name for such writers: unpublished. Now, there's a new word, since they can self-publish: Unsold.

I went after writing success like a poor man with a pickax and one chance to strike gold. Every day I worked at it. I did this because I'd been told years earlier that you couldn't learn to write, you had to be born a writer. I believed it, until I couldn't stand not giving it a try.

I'd been to law school and learned the discipline of concentrated study. I was determined to read books and take classes and show the naysayers I could do it.

I subscribed to *Writer's Digest,* and read Larry Block's fiction column each month as if it were a sacred page.

I joined the Writer's Digest Book Club and built my library. I read and highlighted the books, and took notes on the most important things I was learning.

I then practiced what I'd learned. I showed my stuff to people I trusted and listened to what they said about what wasn't working, and then I went back and figured out how to make it work.

This was virtually every day.

And it was a joy. Learning to improve the thing I loved was never burdensome.

5. Rhino Skin

In the "old days" of the writing business (which means, before 2008), writers really had only one way to a successful career: Convince a publisher to give you money to write for them, and then write for them in a way that makes them money so they can pay you a portion of that money after they have collected on the advance they gave you.

The only way to get a publisher to do that was, usually, by having an agent.

Which gave you two chances at rejection.

The rejection of agents, then the rejection of publishers.

Suppose you got through that thicket? Then you could face the rejection of critics, and after that, the rejection of readers.

And if the readers rejected your book, your publisher could reject your next book, and then your agent might become less than enthusiastic and reject sending your stuff out.

Every rejection was like an arrow to the heart.

Which is why writers had to develop Rhino skin. Novelist Octavia Butler put it nicely when she said, "Let rejection hurt for half an hour, no more. Then get back to your word processor."

Now it is possible to cut out that traditional rejection altogether. It's called self-publishing, and it happens to be covered in the next chapter.

6. Goal Setting

True goals are those to which action may be applied. "I want to be a *New York Times* best-selling author" is not a goal, it's a dream. You can't push a button to make it happen. What you *can* do are the things that will *make you a better writer.* You can determine to spend thirty minutes a day studying craft and an hour a week brainstorming projects. Most of all, you can determine the number of words you will write each week. These are things you can measure and control.

7. Mentored

Mentors can be personal or they can be in print. I consider Larry Block to be a mentor, even though he's never personally coached me. Why? Because I religiously read his monthly *Writer's Digest* column and felt like he was counseling me each time. He had the ability to get into the writer's mind, certainly mine. I try to model my books on the craft after his, or at least I try to write them in the same way.

A good editor, of which there are many out there, can provide mentorship (usually for a fee, which is money well spent when the editor knows what he or she is doing). A good critique partner fits this role as well.

8. Positive

According to an article on the success habits of wealthy individuals,[1] these folks have a positive outlook on life, are upbeat and happy, and grateful for what they have. Some specific findings were as follows:

> 94% are upbeat and happy in terms of their outlook on life
> 98% believed in limitless possibilities and opportunities
> 94% enjoyed their chosen career

Writers, too, need to be grateful that they have the ability to write, and grateful for the opportunity to publish. Further, don't tear down fellow authors. Believe in your limitless choices. Nurture the love of writing that got you started in the first place.

9. Track Progress

The article cited above also found that wealthy individuals were meticulous about measuring how they're doing:

> 67% kept up-to-date to-do lists
> 94% balanced their bank account each month
> 57% counted the calories they consumed
> 62% set goals and tracked whether or not they were on course to achieving them

Remember how I told you that I record the details of my writing sessions on a spreadsheet? I've been doing this since 2001—and you should do the same. That way, you'll know exactly how many words you've spent on what projects, day by week by month by year.

I prioritize my projects and know each day which one I want to work on.

---

[1] http://www.inc.com/jayson-demers/7-habits-of-the-world-s-richest-people.html

However, I don't count my calories. I have determined that eating healthy food does not make you live longer, it only seems longer. (Disclaimer: This is a joke. I am not a doctor, nor do I play one on television.)

10. Associate with Like-Minded People

Dedicate thirty minutes each day to nurturing relationships with other writers. This could mean being a sounding board, giving advice, or just generally being a helpful companion. If you build and nurture relationships, people are likely to reciprocate and become trusted and valuable supporters.

Writers are mostly an encouraging lot. You can find places to hang out with them, starting with a good blog with active comments. Join a local writers group, like an arm of Mystery Writers of America. Go to a good conference.

Systematically disassociate yourself from the sour pickles of life.

Have fun, write, assess, measure, study, correct—then have more fun, write, and never quit. That's a formula for success.

TWENTY-ONE POWER TOOLS FOR TIME MANAGEMENT

1. Plan Your Weeks

The absolute number one rule of time management is you have to plan in advance. And the best way to plan is by the week.

I like to take some time on Sunday and look at the week ahead on the calendar. The first thing I do is mark every block of time where I have an obligation. These things could be work related, family related, whatever.

Once those are marked on the calendar, I'm free to start filling up the rest of the slots with prioritized tasks (see number two). This takes, maybe, five minutes to do, because I already know the tasks I need to perform.

2. Prioritize Your Tasks

Make a list of all the things you want and have to do, a master list of as many things you can think of.

You're going to put these tasks into three different categories.

The first category will feature those tasks that you *must* do. You absolutely have to complete these things in order to accomplish your goals and do your work well.

Put an A next to each item in this category.

Next, look for those important matters that you would *like* to get to if you can. Mark those items with a B.

Finally, select the items on your list that can wait or are optional. Those you mark with the letter C.

Now go through each letter group and prioritize those tasks. For example, your most important A task you will designate as A-1. Your next most important A task is A-2.

Do the same with the Bs and Cs.

Put a time estimate next to each task. If your A-1 task is to complete a report that's due on Friday and you know it's going to take you about two hours, put a 2 next to it. I put my letters at the beginning and my time estimates at the end, like this:

A-1 Finish the report on dental floss distribution. 2
A-2 Start research on new sources of dental floss. 1.5

Once you're used to this process, it becomes simple to do, and the benefits are immediate. You won't have to guess what to schedule for your week, or what task to tackle next during the day. You'll have the plan all set for you.

Be somewhat flexible. If some urgent task pops up, find the right place for it on your list and adjust the other items.

Make a new list every week, eliminating those tasks that no longer apply and adding whatever new ones you need.

3. Take Advantage of Your Best Hour of the Day

Everybody has one hour where they feel the most creative, energetic, sharp, and good-looking. For many, that comes in the morning. For me it's about half an hour into my day, after I've started on that first cup of coffee. I like to wake up early, when it's still dark, and start the coffee going for my wife who is still snoozing away quietly. I then take my cup and go to the computer.

Since I'm a writer, putting down the words is my top priority. I do what I like to call my "nifty 350." That's 350 words typed as quickly as possible, before I do just about anything else. Since I have a daily and weekly quota of words I'm trying to complete, it makes the day go so much more smoothly for me.

Find your own favorite hour. It might be at night when the kids are finally asleep. Or maybe it's when you're at Starbucks at noon and the espresso starts to kick in.

Whatever it is, determine to take full advantage of that hour. Put your head down and work. Do not check your phone or your e-mail. Do not go on Twitter or Facebook. Do not pass Go. Do not collect $200.

You can probably get three times more done in this one hour than you will at any other hour during your day.

4. Do One Thing at a Time

Forget multitasking when you work. Put full concentration on the task at hand.

What you're trying to get to is a sense of *flow*, as described by psychologist Mihaly Csíkszentmihályi in his book of the same name. This is a state of deep, immersive attention. When it happens, you are at your best, mentally and creatively. You know this in part because time seems to speed up, or pass by quickly.

Another term for this state is being in "the zone." You get there by doing just one thing at a time.

5. Take Short Breaks

You can't efficiently concentrate on something indefinitely. Studies show that if you focus hard for about fifty minutes, then take a ten-minute break, your efficiency will optimize. I like to lie on the floor with my feet up, letting the blood flow to my overtaxed gray matter. After ten minutes I pop back up for more work.

If you are at a workplace with a Lumbergh watching you (see the movie *Office Space*), you'll need to find a way to rest your brain for a few minutes.

It's not hard to do.

Sit up straight in your chair, close your eyes, and take five long, slow breaths. As you do, count down from five. Then slowly open your eyes and take one more deep breath. If you can wear headphones and listen to some soft or classical music (or ocean sounds), try that for a few minutes. Imagine you're sitting on a nice beach. Smell the suntan lotion. Feel the breeze.

Also, take your full lunch hour. Don't eat at your desk.

> "Half our life is spent trying to find something to do with the time we have rushed through life trying to save."
> —WILL ROGERS

6. Take a Real Rest One Day a Week

Use one whole day per week for creative leisure. Read. Learn a new subject. Get courses from The Great Courses (an outstanding resource!). But also do this: Use part of the day for pure loafing. That's right. We live in such a hurry-up world. It's possible to fill every second with some sort of activity. Downtime is almost unheard of. We can be Tweeting or Facebooking, texting, or playing Angry Birds or any of an infinite number of games. If you don't learn to shut out the noise for at least part of your week, you'll be more tired and just plain disagreeable than you otherwise might be. And we have to live with you. So loaf.

7. Use a Web-Based Feed Reader to Quickly Go Through Relevant Material

Instead of browsing site by site, set up a feed reader that sends you a digest of chosen content.

I use Feedly.com. It's free and easy to set up. Feedly enables you to pick blogs and feeds that impact your life then sends you headlines to skim. You can read the content if you it looks to be of value.

If you subscribe to printed magazines or newsletters, quickly go over the contents and tear out the articles you want to read. Save those for downtime, when you're waiting in line and the like. Toss the rest of the magazine in the can.

8. Set Aside Time for E-Mail and Social Media

Do not approach these tasks haphazardly. Schedule time for them or they'll suck the time out of you.

9. Put the Boys in the Basement to Work Each Night

Stephen King, one of the best-selling and most prolific writers of all time, has a phrase for the subconscious mind. He calls it "the boys in the basement." He likes it when they send material up to him in the morning. Get into the habit of asking your mind a question before drifting off to sleep. Better yet, write the question on a piece of paper. Be sure to keep a pad and pen handy in case you wake with an insight during the night. Or have your tablet or smartphone ready for a voice recording (this helps if you have lousy handwriting and your midnight notes look like cryptography from the Norwegian Secret Services).

When you wake up in the morning, sit down as soon as possible and record whatever comes to mind. You probably won't use most of it, but there may be nuggets waiting for you that you wouldn't have found otherwise.

10. Learn How to Power Nap

I take a power nap each day during my zombie phase, which is, for me, 2 to 4 P.M. I put my feet up on my desk or go lie down, and am out for fifteen to twenty minutes. That's it. You can learn to do this. It takes a little time, but your body will soon cooperate by sending you quickly to dreamland and waking you up in the allotted time. When I power nap, I get about an hour and a half more productive time in the evening.

After your nap, drink a big glass of water and down a few almonds or walnuts with raisins. I think you'll find, as I do, that this provides a surge of energy and creativity.

11. Throughout the Day Ask, "What's the Best Use of My Time Right Now?"

Every now and then pause in your daily work and ask yourself if what you're doing is the best use of your time. It may very well be. But it could also be that you're spending too much time doing something that doesn't offer enough return.

This doesn't mean you need to be in a constant action mode. Sometimes the best use of your time is a short break.

But by asking yourself this question, and taking perhaps thirty seconds for self-analysis, you'll gain in overall and cumulative productivity.

12. Make Television Your Slave, Not the Other Way Around

DVR news programs so you can whip through them instead of watching them live. Consider doing the same for sports, so you can fast-forward during time-outs and commercials. Make a game of seeing how much television you can do without.

> "Time flies like an arrow. Fruit flies like a banana."
>
> —GROUCHO MARX

13. Reward Yourself when You Have Reached a Significant Milestone

When I finish a manuscript, I like to take a full day off and go on a literary goof. I like the used bookstores in L.A., so I'll start there, browse the shelves, pick up that Cornell Woolrich I've been missing, or add to my collection of 1950s paperback originals. I might just go to a park or the beach, put out a chair and read. That night, I'll take my wife to one of our favorite places for dinner. You simply have to enjoy the journey, or what's the point of it all?

14. Eat a Light Lunch So You Don't Drag in the Afternoon

Salad. Tuna. Chicken. Fruit. These don't drag your brain down into slumber.

Drink plenty of water. You don't have to drown yourself. Six eight-ounce glasses a day seems the operating standard. According to WebMD, even caffeinated drinks—coffee, tea—count. Stay away from sugared drinks.

15. Learn How to Skim Nonfiction Books

The ability to pre-read a nonfiction book saves you time and increases comprehension. Skimming means getting an overview of the book as a whole, starting with the chapter titles, the introduction, and the conclusion of the book. Then, quickly read through the book's chapters, looking at the first paragraphs, any headings, and, if provided, chapter summaries at the end. Once you have a feel for the overall plan of the book, formulate key questions you would like to have answered. Read the book strategically to answer those questions. Rarely do you need to read nonfiction word-for-word, front to back. For example, if you want to know how Andrew Jackson treated Native Americans, and how he changed the presidency, you can skip or quickly scan the parts of his biography that don't apply.

16. Always Have Something to Read for "Waiting" Times

You can always read an e-book on your smartphone. Or you might even carry along a paperback, gasp!

> "Great moments in science: Einstein discovers that time is actually money."
> —GARY LARSON,
> *THE FAR SIDE* CARTOON CAPTION

17. Master 80/20 Thinking

You know the old Pareto Principle: It says that 80 percent of your results come from 20 percent of your activities. Or, the other way around, 20 percent of what you do is going to determine 80 percent of your results. If, for example, you have a list of ten items on your current to-do list, two of them are going to be the most important tasks to perform.

Identify them and do them first.

18. Delegate as Much as You Can

If there is any way to get someone else to perform lower-level tasks for you, even if it costs you a little money, hire them. More and more writers are using virtual assistants (freelancers who work from home) to do things like manage social media, scan e-mails, track sales data, keep a calendar. Save your own time for the most important things you have to do your own sweet self.

19. Handle Each Correspondence Only Once

Be it paper or e-mail correspondence, deal with it only once. If it doesn't demand a response, don't respond.

20. Learn the Art of "Snatching" Time

You can prepare to use "off" times productively. In your car, instead of always listening to music, listen to a self-study course. When you go to the doctor or dentist, bring a project with you. When you fly somewhere, plan to use 80 percent of the flight time doing something productive, not playing games or watching movies.

For long flights I always bring something to edit, something to read, and my computer to write on. I get a window seat so I don't have to get up to let my seat mate use the bathroom.

21. Find Something Higher to Live For

Life is not about you alone. It's about relationships and giving and making the world a better place. The happiest people on earth are those who find a way to give something back. Be one of those people.

> "We are here on Earth to do good to others. What the others are here for, I don't know."
> —W.H. AUDEN

STAY INSPIRED

I'm big on getting inspired. And by that I mean not waiting around for the spirit to move you or the muse to seduce you. Remember Jack London's line: "You can't wait for inspiration. You have to go after it with a club."

To be a professional writer, to be someone who is going to produce work that people want to buy and thus make a living from your writing, you can't afford to wait around. You have to set up a system of work and energy and focus.

Earlier I mentioned a weekly quota. I believe that following through with such discipline, more than anything else, has enabled me to reach whatever writing success I enjoy today. But I don't always want to write. No writer does. There are ebbs and flows in the spirit of the scribe.

But in any endeavor, from athletics to business, those lackadaisical days occur. That's when inspiration becomes an essential. I may be accused of being rah-rah about this, but I don't care. When I was an athlete, I would sit in the locker room psyching myself up for the game.

We know that's all part of it, that's why Knute Rockne became such a legendary football coach. He had the ability to inspire his boys, especially when he urged them to go out there and win one for The Gipper.

They're going to be times when you have to get one for The Gipper, which may just mean getting a page done or a chapter finished.

Collect quotes about writing that inspire you. Turn to them in times of mental fatigue or distress.

And then, the moment you feel a spark, write. This is the most important part.

Write right away.

I've come up with a fake Latin sentiment, giving it to you the way Robin Williams gave it to his students in *Dead Poets Society*:

Carpe Typem!

Seize the keyboard!

A FEW TIPS ON DEFEATING WRITER'S BLOCK

All writers feel "blocked" at one time or another. It comes in varying degrees of severity, but none of it is fatal if you have strategies for overcoming the problem. Here are a few of my favorites.

Get Excited Again

One thing that always gets me ready to write again is rereading portions of my favorite novels. When I take a look at a passage by Raymond Chandler, Michael Connelly, Stephen King, or Charles Dickens, it isn't long before I get pumped up about the very act of writing. We all became writers because we experienced and loved the emotional ride certain books took us on. So re-create that feeling. Reread some favorites and you'll soon want to write again.

Play the Dictionary Game

Take a physical dictionary, yes the actual printed book, and open it up to a random page. Look at the left-hand page and pick the first noun you see. What does that meaning do in your writer's mind? What images does it conjure? How can you integrate whatever you envision into the scene you're working on? You'll be amazed at how often this trick will get you writing again simply by providing a new direction.

Listen to a Great Writer

Here's a technique I picked up from thriller author David Morrell. Imagine that your favorite writer, living or dead, has come up to a cabin in the woods, where you are stalled on your book. While you're sleeping he takes your pages and gives them a read. When you wake up, you find some steaming coffee waiting for you and your favorite writer ready to provide feedback on your current work and how it can get better. It's just a little tweak in your mind, but it opens up new synapses and will create a joyful expectation.

Find Another Spot

Sometimes all you need is a change of scenery to get your mind rolling again. Go somewhere new. Take down some notes about what you observe. Do a little writing exercise where you work your observations into a brand-new scene. Eventually you'll want to get back to your main project again.

Lie Down

Lie down on the floor with your feet up on a chair. Completely relax. Take several deep breaths. Do not think about your book. In your mind, with every breath in, imagine a scoreboard with a big, electric clock on it. The scoreboard begins at 50. With every breath it goes down one number. Countdown to zero. Meanwhile the blood is flowing to your brain and getting all the muck out.

This practice not only reenergizes you, but it gets the creative juices flowing. Dan Brown actually popularized it. He hung upside down between writing stints. You don't have to go that far. Unless you want to.

Move Around

Exercise always helps me. Take a break from your writing and go on a long walk or a bike ride. Or you can simply do thirty seconds of jumping jacks, rest for thirty seconds, and do thirty more seconds of jumping jacks. Repeat three or four times. Now you've got the heart pumping, the blood flowing, and the ideas popping.

The 30K Step Back

I sometimes hit a wall in my first draft around the 30,000-word mark. I don't know why that is, but I have heard other writers tell me they experience the same thing. Maybe it's because you've written an exciting first act and are into Act II, and then you look up and realize you got a heck of a lot of book left to write. Maybe you suffer a crisis of confidence at that point.

Whatever the reason for it, I like to step back and just make sure that my fundamental story structure is sound, and my characters are all operating at their optimum capacity.

Writer's block need never defeat you again. You can trick it, kick it, or run rings around it so long as you remind yourself of two words—just write!

Chapter 8

UNDERSTAND PUBLISHING & MARKETING

Publishing isn't what it used to be. Want to be a successful writer? The way to paying your bills does not run exclusively through New York anymore. You now have the opportunity to carve your own niche. Here's how to sharpen your tools.

FACING DOWN THE HARSH REALITIES OF PUBLISHING

Why doesn't star poker player Phil Ivey get to the final table every year in the World Series of Poker? In fact, why hasn't he ever won the main event? Every observer of the game puts Ivey at the top of the charts in terms of all-around poker skill. He wins a lot of tournaments, but never the big one.

It's because poker isn't only about skill. You've got to get the cards. You can go all in with pocket aces only to see your opponent from Hoboken draw that third eight on the river.

So yeah, it's a mixture of skill and luck. Which pretty much defines any endeavor in life.

Of course, stronger skills increase your odds of success. As one wag put it, "The harder I work, the luckier I get."

In the writing world, especially now, you'll hear a lot about luck and the "harsh reality" of publishing. Whether you're self-publishing, going with a traditional house (large, small, or in-between), or doing a mixture of both, the truth is it's hard to break through and earn big numbers.

If that's the reality of it, then what's the solution? The same answer you'd give anyone starting a business. Do you really want to do this? Are you willing to look reality in the eye and make adjustments? Is this business enough of a passion that you'd do it even if you barely clear your bottom line (e.g., run an independent bookstore)?

Yes? You will keep writing? Even if things are not taking off? Okay.

Keep Your Expectations Low

The great world religions and various schools of philosophy teach that unhappiness comes primarily through *expectations unfulfilled*. Expectations can form images in your mind, such as seeing your e-book hit the Kindle Top 100 list or some such thing. When it doesn't happen, your brain orders a secretion of chemicals that make you feel like pig slop.

Set goals and have dreams, yes, but temper them with the understanding that you're not to depend on them for your happiness. "If you can dream, and not make dreams your master ..." Kipling wrote.

Keep Your Work Ethic High

Get feedback. Read books and articles on writing. Keep learning. Try new things. Experiment with short form. Maybe you'll find a new genre you like and that readers like, too. At the very least, you'll be exercising your skills. Dean Koontz was a middling writer for the first ten years of his career. But he was crazily prolific. And all along the way he taught himself about the craft. When he intentionally took a leap into deeper characterization (with *Whispers*) he shot up another level. And he's had several leaps like that since.

Keep Your Joy Hot

It's always a combination of things that betters your odds. Knowing how to free your voice is one of those things. When you find the joy in your writing, your voice is freed almost automatically. And it's also more fun to write this way. You might as well have fun at this thing.

Keep Your Grumbling Cool

As I've said before, if you get a rejection from a publisher or agent, let it hurt for half an hour, then get back to your keyboard. The same goes for those who self-publish. Your latest release mired in mud? Okay, grouse to somebody about it, or bay at the moon, but then get back to work on your next project.

Keep on Writing for the Rest of Your Life

If you love to write, why would you ever stop? If writing doesn't make a living for you, do it because you love it, and do what you can with it. Keep your day job but find your "quota sweet spot" (the number of words you can comfortably type in a day) and stick to it.

Persistence plus production plus quality improvements lead to success. That's been the formula for business success ever since Eli Whitney. (Did you know the cotton gin didn't make him rich, but muskets did, years later? Well, now you do.)

Let Hugh Howey, the huge self-publishing success, have the last word (from a comment[1] on KBoards.com):

> Which leads to my point of this long-winded nonsense: Time has to be an ingredient. An important one. This [self-publishing] revolution has barely gotten started. Good luck and bad luck require time to even them out. If you've done everything right, your works might take off in ten years. Who knows? We haven't been at this long enough. I think it's too early for any of us to say something isn't working or that it won't work. I just have to remember back to

---

[1] http://www.kboards.com/index.php?topic=164629.msg2361138#msg2361138

writing seven novels over three years and watching them sit between #335,204 and #1,302,490 in the Amazon store. I didn't care. I just kept writing. I read about Amanda Hocking, and I thought: "Hellz yeah!" And I kept writing. I gave myself until I was 40 and I had twenty titles published before I worried about whether I sold enough to pay a bill. And even if that never happened, it was an excuse to publish twenty titles. I could always say that. No one could take it away from me. And anyway, I'd sold a handful of books and heard from people that they loved them. I remembered when that was just an idle dream.

REALITY EXERCISES

1. Do you know the difference between expectations and goals?
2. Dreams should motivate you, but when they become expectations they can debilitate. Write down your dreams. Now write down every action you can take (within your control) toward those dreams. Turn those actions into goals.
3. Eliminate all expectations. Whenever you achieve a goal, celebrate. Then look to your next actions.
4. Remember: Every day you do something that gets you nearer to a goal (whether it's writing, studying, submitting, publishing) is a victory.

A SHORT COURSE ON SUCCESSFUL SELF-PUBLISHING

The self-publishing revolution has spawned a veritable flood of advice, how-tos, blogs, commentary, and hoopla. Below is my overview on the most important things you need to know to get started ... and thrive as a self-publishing writer.

You Must Think Like a Publisher

Supersuccessful indie writer Bella Andre said in an interview, "I have an economics background and I've always been entrepreneurial. This is the perfect sweet spot for me, someone who understands how to run a business, really enjoys building a brand and marketing but also has a deep creative strain."

You can find your own sweet spot if you learn to think like a publisher.

There are three main functions of a publishing house: acquisitions, production, and marketing. Everything a publisher does falls under one of these umbrellas.

You need to think that way, too.

Acquisitions

In a publishing house there are weekly meetings called "pub board." This meeting is usually made up of representatives from editorial and sales, along with the publisher. At this meeting editors present projects they believe the publisher should buy and bring to market.

The editors have to convince sales that the book is commercial enough for the company to make money from it, and that the author is one who deserves their investment.

The editors are always trying to find a "fresh voice." The sales team is always trying to find commercial viability.

So in thinking like a publisher, and considering your own projects, put those two things together: your voice and what has a chance to sell.

Production

When a book goes into production, there is a series of steps the publishing company has long since followed. You need to do the same.

Included in this is a physical print copy of your book. You will want to go through the same quality controls as you prep your print version. I use CreateSpace, Amazon's print-on-demand service, and have been extremely pleased.

Other authors choose to go with a company called "Lightning Source."

Either way, you need a professional-looking layout and print cover. For this, I highly advise you hire the work out to a professional. But you can begin teaching yourself about the important concepts by looking at articles on thebookdesigner.com.

Marketing
Finally, there is a marketing plan for each book. See the following.

You Must Write the Best Books You Can
This means not just writing, but growing as a writer. You should be studying your craft while simultaneously producing your words. See chapter six on studying the craft.

You Must Prepare Your Book with Quality Controls
As Brian Tracy puts it, "The companies with the highest quality are the companies that earn the highest profits. They represent the greatest opportunities for the future."

Remember, you are in business, and you need a checklist for the essential quality factors for your book production.

For self-publishers, this is the list:

1. your writing
2. editing
3. cover design
4. marketing copy
5. formatting
6. distribution

Some writers just want to write. The idea of learning tech stuff fills them with dread.

That's okay. You can simply find people to work with in each of these areas. Using Google and, best of all, recommendations, you can find freelancing professionals and begin to build a team you can rely on.

A word about one-stop services, like BookBaby. For a fee or a percentage, a service like this will distribute your e-book to various online retailers. This is as an alternative to setting up your own accounts with those retailers and uploading the books.

The advantage to the one-stop shop is that you don't have to think about the distribution details. You have one place that distributes and collects the dough and pays you.

On the other hand, you lose some flexibility. If, for example, you want to change the price of a book, it can take weeks to get that to happen.

While the final decision is up to you, I am most in favor of self-publishing writers setting up their own publishing company as a corporation. This is not hard to do. Consider LegalZoom.com as a starting point. In this scenario, you will have direct accounts with the big retailers.

You Must Develop and Work a Marketing Plan

There are mountains of books, blogs, articles, and consultants that offer endless advice on marketing strategies. All this information can be confusing. *What works best? What should I spend my time on? How can I market and write at the same time? What price should I make my books?*

But you have to consider these questions. You need to commit to a written plan and then work at it with good return on investment (ROI).

Start by committing to your craft. Your goal is to become a master. As agent Donald Maass says, "Your best promotion is within the covers of the last book."

This also means that it's going to take you more than one book to gain traction and momentum.

You will need a website that is navigable and has a place where readers can sign up for your e-mail list. You should have a link in the back of all of your e-books that takes people to this sign-up page. Use a company like MailChimp or Vertical Response to store your list and give you HTML for your sign-up forms.

After your book has been out a while and has garnered a number of reviews (twenty is a good benchmark), you can pay for placement in various deal-alert services. This requires that you lower your normal price for a few days so subscribers get your book at a nice discount.

The biggest service right now is BookBub. Options include BookGorilla, eBookSoda and several others. Paying for placement is always worth it, even if you don't break even the first time around. That's because you're paying for readers, a percentage of whom will become repeat customers.

Other strategic opportunities include blog tours, writing guest commentary on blogs, setting up a dynamic Amazon author page, and speaking at local events. But none of them are as good as word of mouth, which is generated by people loving what you write.

Regarding social media, remember that it is about true interaction and community. You build trust that way and network with readers. When you have a book come out, you can certainly mention it, so long as you are not hammering your followers with variations on "Buy my book!"

A Note on Pricing

Choosing the right price for your book is a matter of strategy first and ultimate revenue second.

If you're just getting started, you want to get eyeballs on your pages. One strategy is to price your novel at ninety-nine cents, which gives people low risk for trying you out. You also might want to give the book away for free. One way to do that is via the Kindle Select program, which requires you to be exclusive for a ninety-day term with Amazon.

There is no way to know for certain which is best. It may even vary from book to book.

You simply have to try things and track your sales every month.

You Must Repeat Over and Over for the Rest of Your Life

Self-publishing is a volume business. The more good work you put out there, the better you are going to do.

How good?

It depends. But if you want to start at the top, there is the writer previously mentioned, Bella Andre. She was a traditionally published category romance writer in 2010. She'd done eight books for two different publishers without much financial success.

Self-publishing was just coming into its own, and at a friend's suggestion Andre decided to give it a try.

She uploaded her first e-book, *Love Me,* and priced it at $3.99. In one month she made $20,000, which was four times as much as any book contract she'd ever signed. She put up another e-book a few months later and it became the first self-published title to hit Amazon's Top 25 best-sellers list.

Andre was in the right place at the right time with the right product (romance) and the right work ethic. Between 2010 and 2014, Andre put out thirty, count 'em, thirty! e-books. Her earnings over that time? All she will say is that it is in the "eight figures."

Remember, that is the top of the heap, but it shows you what's possible if you keep on keeping on, and most important, you write well.

In the strata under people like Bella Andre and Hugh Howey are a huge and increasing number of authors who are making fantastic money as writers.

Many more are making enough to quit their day jobs.

Even more than that are making enough for car payments and mortgages, and their kids' educations.

And the great part about being a self-publishing writer is that no one can stop you.

You get to keep going. You get to keep trying. You get to keep getting better. You don't have to sit down with someone telling you you're not capable, that you should just quit, that you should go away and leave your dreams to others. You don't have to take that as long as you've got a keyboard and an imagination.

And in this way, you can never be defeated.

Are you a real writer?

Then keep writing.

And don't stop.

Ever.

THE STRATEGIC USE OF SHORT FICTION

The new world of self-publishing options calls to mind the golden age of the pulp magazines. During that era, roughly 1920–1950, writers could earn decent money pounding out stories and novellas for a penny a word.

Later, the 1950s boom in mass-market paperbacks provided another source of lettuce for the enterprising author. Production and quality were key. If you could deliver the goods on a regular basis, you could actually make a go of the uncertain and unpredictable writer's life.

The same thing is true today.

Many use short-form fiction as a strategic component of building a lasting readership. With e-readers and (increasingly) smartphones used as reading devices, short fiction is once again in demand, as evidenced by venues such as Amazon's Kindle Singles.

The Potential

Hugh Howey, the self-publishing superstar who shot to fame with his Wool series, had no idea what was going to happen when he published the first 12,000-word story on the Kindle platform. "That was it," Howey says. "There was no more story. I made the work available and did zero promotion for it. I thought it was the least commercial of my works, being short and very inexpensive."

But soon *Wool* was outselling all his previous works combined. One thousand copies in a month, three thousand the next, and ten thousand the month after that.

Howey knew he had a hit on his hands. "I heeded the flood of e-mails and reviews," he says, "and started writing the next part."

The rest is well-known in the indie world. *Wool* was optioned for film by Ridley Scott. A print-only deal with Simon & Schuster followed. Howey retained the right to publish the e-books on his own.

There is always the chance that a good series of short fiction will catch on and become a solid income stream. But that's not the only reason to pursue short-form work.

Prolific writer Kristine Kathryn Rusch, who makes good money from short stories, also uses them to help create and enhance her full-length fiction. "I explore the worlds of my novels," she says. "If I introduce a major new character, I write a short story to figure out who that character is."

Rusch also uses her short work to find new readers. She'll take a story that is normally for sale online and make it free for a week. "I put up a free short story every Monday and take that story down the following Monday. Free, one week only. And boy, has that grown my blog's readership, and my own."

The Forms

Short-form fiction is anything less than a novel. The minimum word count for a novel varies, depending on genre, audience, and (as with many things in publishing today) whom you ask, but is usually tagged at 50,000. Below that, you have the following, with slight variations of opinion:

Novella

Between 20,000 and 50,000 words, the novella was a popular form in the age of the pulps because it could take up most of a magazine and leave readers feeling like they got a good story for their money.

But when the pulps dried up, so did novellas. Though a title occasionally broke through (e.g., *The Bridges of Madison County*) or was included in a collection of short fiction by a single author, most traditional publishers did not find novellas cost-effective to produce.

Now the novella is back and self-publishers—who don't need to worry about things like print runs and page signatures where e-books are concerned—are releasing them in droves.

A novella works best when it has one main character and one main plot. An example is James M. Cain's classic crime novella *The Postman Always Rings Twice*. Coming in at just under 40,000 words, it's a love-triangle-leads-to-murder story. It has the famous opening line: *They threw me off the hay truck about noon.*

The story is told in first-person narration by Frank Chambers. But novellas work equally well in third-person point of view.

Other famous novellas include:

- *The Pearl*, John Steinbeck
- *The Old Man and the Sea*, Ernest Hemingway
- *A Christmas Carol*, Charles Dickens
- *Rita Hayworth and the Shawshank Redemption*, Stephen King
- *The Escape Route*, Rod Serling
- *A River Runs Through It*, Norman Maclean

Novelette

Not quite so well-known is the novelette. At between 7,000 and 20,000 words, it allows for a little more breathing space than a short story without requiring the fuller complexity of a novel.

A novelette, like its beefier cousin the novella, is best when it's about one main character and story. Novelettes are perhaps best known in the sci-fi world. Howey's original *Wool*, for example, was novelette length. The Science Fiction & Fantasy Writers of America give an annual Hugo Award in this category. Perhaps you've heard of some of the other famous winners:

- Philip K. Dick, "Faith of Our Fathers"
- Harlan Ellison, "Basilisk"
- Orson Scott Card, "Ender's Game" (later expanded into a novel)

Short Story

An enduring and popular form, the short story can pack an emotional punch as powerful as a novel. At 1,000–7,000 words in length, the best stories usually revolve around *one shattering moment.*

The shattering moment can come at the beginning of the story with the consequences played out (e.g., "A Candle for the Bag Lady" by Lawrence Block); or it can come at the end, usually as part of an intriguing plot that has a surprise ending. A master of this form is Jeffery Deaver (see his collections *Twisted* and *More Twisted).*

And, yes, the shattering moment can be in the middle, as in Raymond Carver's classic "Will You Please Be Quiet, Please?"

Flash Fiction

Usually under 1,000 words, flash fiction is a world of its own. You can explore many venues for this type of work online.

The Strategies

Short-form fiction published as independent, stand-alone works should not be viewed (at least initially) as a source of major self-publishing profits. That's because to remain competitive on Amazon, Barnes & Noble, Kobo, and other retailers, you have to price them at the lower end—usually for ninety-nine cents or for free. Pricing is not a science, so you should experiment. A novella might support a price of $2.99 or even more on occasion. It takes several months to a year of conducting pricing/promotional experiments and collecting data to figure out what's working best for you.

Here are some other strategic uses of short fiction:

USE THEM IN THE KINDLE SELECT PROGRAM. Kindle Select is a program Amazon offers under the Kindle Direct Publishing umbrella. By giving Amazon exclusive distribution rights (in ninety-day increments), you can offer a work for free for five days. Those days can be spaced apart or used all at once. For all of the rest of the days in this period, your story will be priced as usual.

My preference is to use all five days in a row and to get the word out on social media. The goal is to get eyeballs on the story and to make new readers who will then want to seek out your full-length books. If you don't yet have any full-length books to offer, these free looks can begin to build your readership with your readers.

USE YOUR STORIES AS FREE GIVEAWAYS WHEN PEOPLE SIGN UP FOR YOUR NEWSLETTER. Successful independent writers know that the two best marketing tools are word of mouth and an e-mail list of readers. To start building that list, many authors include a sign-up form on their blog or website. When a person signs up, a free story or book is sent to them.

I recommend using at least a novelette-length story for this—make sure it's a good one. You not only want those sign-ups, you also want readers who will become fans.

USE THEM AS SERIALS. Using a model from the good old days, many writers are now serializing their novels. They publish in installments and charge a low price. Some authors refer to this as episodic fiction, likening it to a television series such as *Lost* or *True Detective*.

Later, as Hugh Howey did with *Wool*, you can gather the series into one volume. But also heed Howey's advice: "I think it's a bad idea to simply chop up a novel into shorter pieces. Each work needs to satisfy on its own."

Howey emphasizes that each piece "should have its own beginning, middle, and end. Cliff-hangers work only if the protagonists have overcome some other obstacle along the way. Don't string your readers along; invite them back for more."

USE THEM TO PROMOTE A NEW NOVEL. A few years ago, the big publishing houses started commissioning short works from their A-list authors. Lee Child, Michael Connelly, and Janet Evanovich—just to name a few—put out shorts featuring their popular series characters. Doing so not only helped promote their next novels, but also kept their readers engaged during those in-between periods.

USE THEM TO KEEP YOUR JOY ALIVE. Sometimes you need to write something just for the fun of it. This keeps your writing chops sharp and your writer's soul soaring. That's how it was with my short story "Golden." It's not my usual thriller or noir beat, but it was a story I needed to write. It makes me happy that it's out there—and that readers have found it.

"If you like to read short stories, write them," Rusch says. "It's that simple. Write what you love. That's really the most important thing—and believe it or not, the most important thing to making a living."

USE THEM TO INCREASE YOUR CHANCES OF SUCCESS. If there's one consistent drumbeat coming from successful indie authors, it is that they believe production is key. And that's not surprising, considering it's similar to the thinking that occurred during the pulp era I talked about earlier in this chapter. One of those great pulp writers, Edgar Rice Burroughs, once said, "If you write one story, it may be bad; if you write a hundred, you have the odds in your favor."

THE END OF DISCOVERABILITY
AND THE RISE OF MERIT

One of the long-term consequences of the digital revolution is, of course, the decline of physical bookstores. Remember when there were at least two or three great bookstores in town? There were more in a big city, with a lot of indies to choose from, as well as the chains. I remember Pickwick, which was bought out by B. Dalton, which was bought out by Barnes & Noble.

There was Brentano's, which was acquired by Waldenbooks, which was acquired by K-Mart, and rolled over into Border's.

Then, all of a sudden, there was no more Border's.

And now poor Barnes & Noble is the last chain standing. But it's been closing stores left and right. Its CEO was ousted. The future of its remaining brick-and-mortar outlets is cloudy at best. Which of course ripples upward to the traditional publishers.

We all should have bought Proctor & Gamble stock in 2007, when the Kindle hit the market, because P&G makes Pepto-Bismol. Sales of the pink elixir must have shot through the roof in publishing boardrooms across Manhattan.

All of which leads us to another consequence of monumental importance: the end of discoverability.

What do I mean? Take a look at these stats from an article in *Salon.com* (July 19, 2013):

> According to survey research by the Codex Group, roughly 60 percent of book sales—print and digital—now occur online. But buyers first discover their books online only about 17 percent of the time. Internet booksellers specifically, including Amazon, account for just 6 percent of discoveries. Where do readers learn about the titles they end up adding to the cart on Amazon? In many cases, at bookstores.
>
> The brick and mortar outlets that Amazon is imperiling play a huge role in driving book sales and fostering literary culture. Although beaten by the Internet in unit sales, physical stores outpace virtual ones by 3-to-1 in introducing books to buyers. Bookshelves

sell books. In a trend that is driving the owner of your neighborhood independent to drink, customers are engaging in "showrooming," browsing in shops and then buying from Amazon to get a discount. This phenomenon is gradually suffocating stores to death. If you like having a bookseller nearby, think carefully before doing this. Never mind the ethics of showrooming—it's self-defeating. You're killing off a local business you like. (If you prefer e-reading, many independent stores have agreements with Kobo and Zola Books that give them a cut of e-book sales.)

As online sales continue to gain ground and shelf space diminishes, "discoverability" has become a big worry-word in the industry. To make a point so obvious that it's sometimes overlooked, the most crucial moment in bookselling is the moment a reader finds out that a book that sounds interesting *exists*. How else is she going to buy it?

So there you have it. Physical bookstores are (were?) the big driver of discoverability. Shoppers walked in and saw a huge front-of-the-store display of a writer the publisher put big bucks behind. They saw recommendations from store staff, and the covers of certain titles displayed with full cover showing. They saw all sorts of books in all sorts of ways.

But when that space is no longer there, what happens to discoverability?

Well, you can try to create a new stream. A newly implanted CEO of a big publisher says the major houses are the ones who will be able to "crack the code of discoverability in a world of fewer bookstores, to come closer to the end consumer, to keep readers more interested in reading and provide them with the best reads."

To which I say, with all due respect, *there is no code to be cracked*. There never was. Once upon a time there was but one system with but one player: the publishers, who controlled placement in bookstores.

But the era of massive placement is over. What do we have instead? An old-fashioned system, one your grandparents called *merit*. That means trust, which is *earned*, over time, as people come to rely on the quality of your offerings.

This is good news for writers. Because it *should* be about the writing, and writing is a craft, and craft can be learned, and writers can get better.

In the past, writers needed the backing of a big publisher to get any prominent real estate in a store. Precious few writers ever got the royal treatment. But now the playing field is digital. And those who compete directly for reader loyalty do so with *the same chance to grab market share as anyone else.*

Thus the key to success in this game is not advertising, shelf space, co-op, *The New York Times*, algorithm ping-pong, bookstore signings, launch parties, or social media saturation. It is simply and reliably this: producing good book after good book.

Sure, you need a home base (website) and a modicum of exposure to social media. You have to give some thought to how you present your professional self to the world. You'll have to explore means of "getting the word out" when you have a book available.

But all that pales in comparison to the most crucial factor, now and forevermore: the quality of the experience you deliver to readers. Concentrate on that and discoverability will take care of itself.

WE ARE ALL LONG TAIL MARKETERS NOW

The traditional book publishing industry, God bless it, may be hacking and wheezing like characters in the last act of *La Bohéme*. I wish it were not so, as it is a good thing to have printed, bound volumes of paper books for those who prefer that medium. But as Dr. House is wont to say, "Tragedies happen."

For writers of any stripe—be they independent, traditional, or hybrid—now is the time to step away from Mimi and her coughing fit for a moment and take the long view. And that's where we see the long tail.

What is "long tail marketing"? Very simply, it holds that the profitability of small business is directly proportional to the number of products it has for sale over time. The more products (factoring in quality, of course), the longer the tail. Instead of looking for the next big thing, a business may sell "less of more."

Old school thinking focuses on the launch. The front list. The blockbuster. The big rollout. Backlist is largely left alone, except for heavy hitters who get the shelf space in the bookstores.

Self-publishing writers, the ones who are making some good money at it, go at it the other way. Volume is the key. That's what wags the long tail.

Traditional publishing is beginning to recognize this, and thus is asking its A-list writers to produce more, faster, and even to supplement their front list with shorter works.

In other words, we are all long tail marketers now.

Many self-publishing writers miss this, however. I hear and read laments from writers starting to self-publish that haven't seen big sales. They think that means failure. But that's old school thinking. It's not about a title or two spiking its way up the Kindle list a month after release. That's nice when it happens, but the real meat is in the long tail. And what is the long tail? It's adding more product over the course of time.

As I like to say, the final "law" of success in this writing game is to repeat the production-publication cycle over and over for the rest of your life. Why not? If you're a writer, this is what you do until you can't do it anymore, right?

Yes, you need quality control. That's a law, too. But here's another aspect of the long tail: Single title duds are not fatal to a career. All writers in the traditional world know that they are only a dud or two away from being unemployed. Tales of authors getting nice advances, having the books disappoint the sales department, getting dropped by their publisher, and not being able to find another because of lousy numbers are innumerable.

Self-publishing with a long tail is the reverse of that scenario. If a book or two is a dud, it doesn't mean that you can't produce a better book next time. You can even remove the dud and redo it if you like.

Also, you can try out new niches for a spot on the long tail. In old school thinking, you are tied to a single brand. In the new school, you can play. You can create works of any length. You can start a series based on a lark and let the readers decide if it continues. And here's another factor: There is no huge up-front cost to publishing like this. Even something that doesn't sell well will make you Starbucks money eventually. No harm, no foul.

Some other things the long tail method brings to the table are listed below:

- You don't need to win awards.
- You don't need the approval of critics.
- You don't need to be number one on any list.
- You don't need a movie deal.

What you need is optimism, a work ethic, and consistency. Then you will grow an audience that is fitted for *you*. You might even make a living at this eventually. But even if it's only a moderate stream of income, that's a nice thing to have feeding your bank account every month.

Think long term, long tail. And keep writing.

MARKETING LESSONS MY GRANDFATHER TAUGHT ME

My grandfather, Arthur Scott Bell, was born in 1890. He grew up in Ann Arbor, Michigan, where he was an outstanding athlete for Ann Arbor High.

He won an athletic scholarship to DePauw University, later transferring to the University of Michigan to play football. He joined the Army in World War I, and during that time he met my grandmother, Dorothy Fox. One of the treasure troves I have is the box of love letters he wrote to her from Fort Sheridan, Illinois. My grandmother kept them all, bound with ribbons. When my father was little, he'd hear his father call his mother Dot, and he combined that with Mama, so ever after my grandmother was known as Mama Dot. Later on, my dad started calling his father Padre.

And that's how all his grandkids knew him.

One of Padre's favorite phrases was, "Go your best." He said that to me a number of times—when I was off to a new school year, or starting Little League.

During the Great Depression, Padre fed his family as a field salesman for the *Encyclopedia Britannica*. He was a stellar salesman, rising to become one of the top ten in the entire company.

From what Padre and my dad told me about those days, I gathered five lessons that apply to writers (and anyone else) trying to peddle their wares.

He Believed in His Product

Padre loved the *Britannica*. I have a full set from 1947, passed down to me. (Note: If you have one, don't get rid of it. The entries in these volumes are often better and more authoritative than anything you can find today.)

Do you believe in your product? Are you convinced that what you're writing is the best you can make it? Or are you going out there with something less than that—and still expecting good sales?

He Believed in Self-Improvement

Padre was a lifelong learner. On my shelf I have Padre's dictionary, the *Webster's New Collegiate, 2nd Edition*. In the front of the dictionary, on one of the blank pages, Padre had written himself a note on a new word: *psycho-cybernetics*. That would place this note around 1960, when the book by Maxwell Maltz first came out. Padre was seventy years old then but still interested in growing his vocabulary.

He was of the Dale Carnegie school of self-improvement. Another treasure I own is the hardcover copy of *How to Win Friends and Influence People* that Padre and Mama Dot gave my dad upon his graduation from Hollywood High School. They each inscribed it. Padre wrote the following:

> To have a friend is to be a friend. I am sure you are getting to be an expert at it. Don't let down!!

And from Mama Dot:

> You can do more than strike while the iron is hot. You can make the iron hot by striking.

Are you growing as a writer? Are you spending some part of your week in purposeful study of the craft? Padre and Mama Dot's generation believed anyone could succeed if they studied and worked hard enough.

He Concentrated on the Best Prospects

Padre had a definite strategy when he pulled into a new town. He looked up all the lawyers and doctors. These would be the people most likely to have some disposable income during the Depression. Thus they would be the most likely to buy.

Simple enough. But when it comes to marketing, how many writers out there are trying to cast a wide net in the hope of snagging some random fish? The difference between 100,000 low-engagement followers and 10,000 quality followers is huge. Don't try to be all things to all people, but be a value add-on for those who most likely want to sample your work. When you blog or tweet, do it with your specific audience in mind. What interests *them?* Write about those things and link to that content.

He Made People Feel Good

My grandfather was a natural storyteller. He had a deep, resonant voice. I can hear it now. And when he started spinning a tale, you sat mesmerized.

I remember one story he told about a football player at Michigan named Molbach. The fellows called him "Molly." He was a fullback, a powerhouse runner who could not be stopped in short yardage situations. Padre told about one tough game where Molly put his head down and ran so hard he kept going over the sideline and ran right into a horse—and knocked the horse down!

Padre's storytelling made you feel good. He brought you into the moment. The legend in the family was that Padre had a story for every occasion.

Does your marketing make people feel good? If someone sees your tweets or Facebook posts, will they generally be pleased with what you've posted? Or do you depend on a barrage of useless "buy my book" type messages?

Work at making your social media a pleasure for others to read. "To have a friend is to be a friend."

He Could Laugh at Life

Padre was a man "at home in his own skin." He'd been through plenty in his life, the Depression not least among them. But he always came out all right in the end.

He had the greatest laugh in the world. It came from deep in his chest and rumbled out in joyous reverberation.

Remember that you need to be able to laugh. And in order to laugh, you can't be constantly stressing over outcomes and expectations. If you follow Padre's lessons, you'll work hard on yourself and your writing. You'll be smart about marketing and refuse to let setbacks stop you. You simply won't worry about the things that are outside of your control.

Manage your expectations; don't let them rule you. Concentrate on what you can do, not what is out of your hands.

Strike the iron.

Keep writing.

Go your best.

MARKETING IS EASY, WRITING IS HARD

It was probably the English actor Edmund Kean (1787–1833) who uttered famous last words that have been attributed to others. On his deathbed he was asked by a friend if dying was hard. The thespian replied, "Dying is easy. Comedy is hard."

Let's adapt this to fit our lives as writers: Writing is hard. You should know that already. (I should say "writing *well* is hard," but that doesn't sound as snappy.)

But here's the other side: Marketing is easy.

Yes, I said easy. I can hear the sighs, nay, the *howls* of protest. "If it's so easy, how come my books aren't selling?"

The answer is almost always: Because writing is hard. You've got to have a superior product to sell, and that's not easy. It's not easy for any business to create great products. If it were, everybody would be a business success.

Believe me when I say it takes quality production that you repeat, over and over, for the rest of your life, to make a go of independent publishing.

So why am I saying marketing is easy? Because marketing is not the same as that tiresome buzzword, *discoverability*. If you remember that, your life will be a lot happier. Write well, and market easily, and discovery takes care of itself. In fact, that's the only way it gets taken care of at all.

You see, the marketing venues that work best for fiction writers are now pretty much settled. In my opinion, these are the top five:

Word of Mouth

This is, has been, and always will be the greatest driver of sales for any novelist. It is "passive marketing," because others do the promoting on your behalf.

Beyond the book itself, you really cannot do anything to improve word of mouth. Some authors attempted to do so a few years ago, by buying five-star reviews. But that practice quickly flamed, and some authors suffered because of it.

So don't stress about this aspect of marketing. But in the words of Bonnie Raitt, give 'em something to talk about.

Your Own Mailing List

Growing a list should be one of your ongoing enterprises. You should have a website with a place for readers to sign up for your updates. You should also learn how to communicate effectively so as not to annoy people. Don't make your communication to your list just a "please buy my book" appeal. Make your notifications a pleasure to read. For example, I always try to include one fun fact or laugh line in my e-mails. And I keep it short!

Kindle Direct Publishing Select

As I mentioned earlier in the chapter, if you're just starting out, the Select program from Kindle Direct Publishing (KDP) is one of the best ways to get your work out to new readers. You list your book exclusively with the Kindle store for ninety days and are allowed to offer your book free for five days within that period. The days can be used singly or in order. I advise using the days consecutively, as I mentioned previously.

How you utilize KDP Select with multiple titles is up to you, but I would advise keeping at least some short fiction works with the program. You can use free promotion to introduce new readers to your writing.

A Subscriber-Based Ad

Services like BookBub, BookGorilla, and Kindle Nation Daily may run an ad for your book. You pay for the privilege. But here is where many writers make a mistake. You should not view this kind of ad as a way to make money or "break even." You may, in fact, not make back your initial investment.

But it's still worth it because when you attract new readers, a percentage of them will become repeat customers. Thus the value of your return is not dollar for dollar, but future income based upon the new readers you generate.

Some Social Media Presence

It's necessary to have some footprint out there in social media. But don't try to do everything. Pick something you enjoy and that doesn't gobble up too much of your time. Remember, social media is about "social" and not (primarily) about selling. There is a part of social media that's too hard for me to recommend: personal blogging. I participate in a group blog. Trying to produce content by myself, at least three times a week, takes too much time and effort for too little return. The people who can do this are few, and I'm still not convinced the return on energy (ROE) is worth it. Choose wisely where you specialize.

The Actual Writing

Now the hard part, writing. Concentrate most of your efforts here. Writing is a craft. It has to be learned, practiced, polished, criticized, revised, and practiced some more. It has to be wild and free on one side, yet disciplined and structured on the other.

Yes, you can write for pure pleasure, that's fine. You don't have to sell in big numbers if you don't want to. But if you're serious about gathering readers in ever increasing numbers, work at the craft.

Beethoven had to work at his music.

Picasso had to work at his painting.

Pete Rose had to work at baseball. He became one of the greatest hitters of all time with less than all-time talent. His problem was that he thought gambling was easy.

So here is your lesson for publishing: Work on your writing and don't gamble.

HOW NOT TO FUMBLE YOUR SOCIAL MEDIA PRESENCE

Seth Godin, whom many consider the premiere social media guru, uttered a word of caution to traditional book publishers at the Digital Book World conference:

> The challenge we have is not all of your authors want to be good at social media. And not all of them have something to say when they're not writing a book. Is the only way to sell books to dance faster than everyone else? I don't think it is. ... What we have to figure out is not merely does this author have 70,000 good words to say in a row, but do they have a following, can we help them get a following, are they the kind of person where a reader says, "I can't wait for your next work."[2]

The prevailing wisdom about social media has coalesced around the fact that it is best for forming community and only marginally effective for selling things like books. A good social media presence (henceforth referred to as SMP) certainly can help with a launch if—and this is crucial—you have established trust by consistently offering quality content to your followers.

On the other hand, abusing your SMP can render the whole thing a complete waste of time.

What do I mean by abuse? I call it the Ned Ryerson Syndrome. You remember Ned, from the great comedy *Groundhog Day*. He was the insurance salesman who accosted Bill Murray in each

---

[2] Quoted by Jane Friedman (https://janefriedman.com/ebooks-print-market/)

reload of the day, until finally Murray just punches him in the face before he can get a word out.

What does Ned do wrong? Count the ways! He demands attention. He exhibits lousy communication skills. He makes lame jokes. Worst of all, without an invitation, he pushes his product into Bill Murray's face and keeps on doing it.

I like to do a little personal research on this issue every now and then. The way it happens is that I'll come across an indie author I don't know but who looks interesting. Most of the time it's because a nice book cover catches my eye. I'll click to see if that author has other books, and what the general reviews and ranking are. Then I'll check on his SMP.

For example, I've had the following situation occur. I noticed a really nice thriller cover from an author I hadn't heard of. He had three other nice thriller covers. But his Amazon rankings were not good for any of the titles. He had a handful of reviews that averaged out to ... average.

Now, I believe the books themselves always have the most to do with any of this. But there may be other reasons a book or series doesn't take off.

I checked this author's SMP, starting with his Twitter account. And boy, did I find Ned Ryerson.

Not one of his tweets contained content or attempted to interact with others. Every single one was some sort of sales pitch. There were different kinds of pitches: a *deal* kind, then a *line from the book* kind, followed by a *book cover* kind, and an *elevator pitch* kind. All with links to sales pages.

Over on Facebook, I saw more of the same.

This author was not only wasting his time, he was hurting his prospects. He was making everyone who follows him feel like Bill Murray in his eternal recurrence: *Oh boy, here comes Ned Ryerson again! Do I have to live this moment over and over?*

Remember, the last time Murray sees Ned he just punches Ned in the face.

Here's the SMP lesson of the day: Don't make people want to punch you in the face.

1. Be the Kind of Guest People Want to Have at Their Next Party

What kind of guest is that? One who brings something to a social gathering that people like. Be a content provider. A person who says things that bring a smile, a new thought, or a helping hand.

2. Be Patient

Don't run up to people and yell. Grow naturally.

3. Be Real, But Don't Be a Boor

Honestly, didn't your mother teach you not to say the first thing that pops into your head?

> "Better to remain silent and be thought a fool than to speak out and remove all doubt."
> —ABRAHAM LINCOLN.

4. Go 90/10 on Your Socializing/Selling Ratio

When you launch a book or announce a deal, do so via your SMP. But make sure such things are only about 10 percent of your messaging. That's my unofficial anecdotal rule of thumb.

ANALYZING BOOK DESCRIPTION COPY

One of the key elements of selling online these days is the ability to write book descriptions that sizzle and do the job in three paragraphs or so. In this age of short attention spans, you can't afford to waste any space.

For amusement, I randomly looked at some descriptions (sometimes called "cover copy") from best-selling authors. You ought to do the same. Go through Amazon and study the best books in your genre. See what professional marketing people have come up with. Figure out what works and doesn't work for you. Then write your own copy accordingly.

Here are my thoughts on three book descriptions:

Innocence by Dean Koontz

> He lives in solitude beneath the city, an exile from society, which will destroy him if he is ever seen.
>
> She dwells in seclusion, a fugitive from enemies who will do her harm if she is ever found.
>
> But the bond between them runs deeper than the tragedies that have scarred their lives. Something more than chance—and nothing less than destiny—has brought them together in a world whose hour of reckoning is fast approaching.
>
> In *Innocence*, #1 *New York Times* best-selling author Dean Koontz blends mystery, suspense, and acute insight into the human soul in a masterfully told tale that will resonate with readers forever.

MY SCORE: B-

The first line is pretty good. It captures my attention, and makes me want to read the next line (which is the whole secret of copywriting).

But that second line is a bit soft. I would change "do her harm" to "kill her."

The third paragraph is ambiguous. I'm not sure why I should care that these two people have a "bond." The second line is rather ponderous to get through and has no real specificity. What sort of "reckoning" are we talking about here? Why are these two people involved?

The last line, of course, is puffery for the author. If you're Dean Koontz, you deserve it. But even here, such effusions as "will resonate with readers forever" may be over the top. My advice for us mere mortals: Do not use any of that kind of fluff. You can mention kudos, but only if you back it up with something like a nice blurb from a well-known writer or a review from a trusted source. I don't care how good your self-published thriller is, it is not going to "leave readers transformed forever and change the course of history for all mankind."

NYPD RED 2 by James Patterson & Marshall Karp

NYPD Red—the task force attacking the most extreme crimes in America's most extreme city—hunts a killer who is on an impossible mission.

A vigilante serial killer is on the loose in New York City, tracking down and murdering people whose crimes have not been punished. The number of victims grows, and many New Yorkers secretly applaud the idea of justice won at any price.

NYPD Red Detective Zach Jordan and his partner Kylie MacDonald are put on the case when a woman of vast wealth and even greater connections disappears. Zach and Kylie have to find what's really behind this murderer's rampage while political and personal secrets of the highest order hang in the balance. But Kylie has been acting strange recently—and Zach knows whatever she's hiding could threaten the biggest case of their careers.

NYPD Red 2 is the next spectacular novel in James Patterson's newest series, a book that proves "there's no stopping his imagination." (*New York Times Book Review*)

MY SCORE: A-

This copy starts with a "headline" style, which is often a good idea, but only if the headline is short and to the point. Here, I would take out the whole parenthetical statement and leave this: *NYPD Red hunts a killer who is on an impossible mission.*

The next two paragraphs are excellent. They are specific and to the point and tell me exactly what type of story this is. It has both outer plot (serial killer) and inner journey (Kylie has been acting strange recently). It's all there.

The puffery about Patterson is, of course, also well deserved. Notice that it is backed up with a clip from a trusted source.

Stand Up Guy by Stuart Woods

> **Stone Barrington is back in the newest edge-of-your-seat adventure in the *New York Times*–bestselling series.**
>
> Stone Barrington's newest client does not seem the type to bring mayhem in his wake. A polite, well-deported gentleman, he comes to Stone seeking legal expertise on an unusual—and potentially lucrative—dilemma. Stone points him in the right direction and sends him on his way, but it's soon clear Stone hasn't seen the end of the case. Several people are keenly interested in this gentleman's activities and how they may relate to a long-ago crime ... and some of them will stop at nothing to find the information they desire.
>
> On a hunt that leads from Florida's tropical beaches to the posh vacation homes of the Northeast, Stone finds himself walking a tight-rope between ambitious authorities and seedy lowlifes who all have the same prize in their sights. In this cutthroat contest of wills, it's winner-takes-all ... and Stone will need every bit of his cunning and resourcefulness to be the last man standing.

MY SCORE: B-

The headline focuses on the series character, which is fine. Readers of the series will want to know about it. "Edge-of-your-seat adventure" is a cliché, of course. I wonder if readers have a slightly negative reaction to such things, even subconsciously. Maybe it doesn't matter. I'm not sure. What are your thoughts on it?

The first paragraph is problematic. What is a "well-deported" gentleman? I'm not even sure that's a grammatically correct use of the word *deported,* which itself is archaic. *Key copyrighting tip:* Don't make readers work hard! Write in such a way that a middle school student could read the copy and not get tripped up by any of it.

Also, is there enough at stake here? Why should I care that some people are "keenly interested" in this gentleman's activities? It's also a bit too long for a cover copy paragraph. I'd break it up into two.

The second paragraph gets us a little closer to specifics and how they involve the lead character. I'm okay with that.

And here's one for a short story:

> Sometimes, comedy can seem like death …
>
> For Pete "The Harv" Harvey, stand up comedy is a serious business. At least, he wants it to be. But the struggle to make it in the glitter dome of L.A. hasn't exactly been a smashing success.
>
> One night, after bombing onstage at a local club, Pete wonders if his next stop is managing a car wash. Then a man sits next to him at the bar—a man with an almost unbelievable proposition. One that could mean a whole lot of money to Pete "The Harv" Harvey, who will soon learn that deals too good to be true are no laughing matter.

I think the author, James Scott Bell, did okay with that. It's brief and to the point, gives the setup and then gets out of the way. But in the interest of fairness to the other students, he will not give himself a grade!

Measure your own book descriptions against those written by professionals. You can find them by browsing any online bookstore.

A FINAL NOTE ON THE WRITING LIFE

So what, in the end, is the writing life?

It's romantic, but also hardheaded.

It's fulfilling, though sometimes heartbreaking.

It's something you can do like an assembly line worker—think Charlie Chaplin in *Modern Times*, standing at the moving belt making the same wrench moves over and over again.

Or it's something you can do like Cary Grant seducing Ingrid Bergman in *Notorious*. Or Elizabeth Taylor making eyes at Montgomery Clift in *A Place in the Sun*.

It can be a job. And there's nothing wrong with that. John Cheever would put on a suit and tie in his New York apartment, take the elevator to the basement where he had a writing space, and write.

John D. MacDonald would write until five p.m. and then knock off for martinis.

You can make it a life of self-expression, of getting your ideas down because you desperately want someone to read them.

You can even write for yourself alone and leave your collected works to an executor.

You can write for money. You can write for love.

You can write for mone *and* love.

Whatever you choose, do one thing for me, will you?

Honor the craft.

That means giving a rip about good writing. It means trying to get better at what you do. It means spending some time in study and reflection on what makes writing great. And then trying to do those things in your own writing.

Put passion and craft together. It's unbeatable.

Write hot, revise cool.

The great Ray Bradbury, in *Zen in the Art of Writing*, says:

> Zest. Gusto. How rarely one hears these words used. How rarely do we see people living, or for that matter, creating by them. Yet if I were asked to name the most important items in a writers make-up, the things that shape his material and rush him along the road to where he wants to go, I can only warn him to look to his zest, see to his gusto.

Zest, gusto, joy. These are necessary conditions for a great writing life. But to zest, gusto, and joy you must add the shaping of words, the skill of plot and character, of scene and dialogue.

Fall in love with your writing each day. But plan some trips with a map, too.

When you write, write as if it were impossible to fail. When you revise, revise as if your groceries depended on it.

Write like a wind tunnel. Edit like a vacuum cleaner.

Write like there's no tomorrow. Edit tomorrow.

Write like you're in love. Edit like you're in charge.

I like what Brenda Ueland says in *If You Want to Write*:

> Mentally (at least three or four times a day) thumb your nose at all know-it-alls, jeerers, critics, doubters ... Work from now on, until you die, with real love and imagination and intelligence. If you are going to write you must become aware of the richness in you and come to believe in it and know it is there.

It's there, the richness. It's in you.

Let it out.

Just write.

INDEX